D1299576

Miguel de Cervantes

THE GREAT HISPANIC HERITAGE

Miguel de Cervantes

Cesar Chavez

Frida Kahlo

Juan Ponce de León

Diego Rivera

Pancho Villa

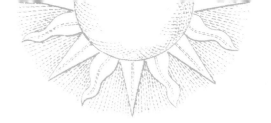

THE GREAT
HISPANIC HERITAGE

Miguel
de Cervantes

Barbara Keevil Parker
and
Duane F. Parker

CHELSEA HOUSE
PUBLISHERS
A Haights Cross Communications ✦ Company
Philadelphia

To Pam, Loern, and Nolan.
May you live your dreams.

CHELSEA HOUSE PUBLISHERS
VP, NEW PRODUCT DEVELOPMENT Sally Cheney
DIRECTOR OF PRODUCTION Kim Shinners
CREATIVE MANAGER Takeshi Takahashi
MANUFACTURING MANAGER Diann Grasse

Staff for MIGUEL DE CERVANTES
ASSISTANT EDITOR Kate Sullivan
PRODUCTION EDITOR Jaimie Winkler
PHOTO RESEARCHER Noelle Nardone
SERIES & COVER DESIGNER Terry Mallon
LAYOUT 21st Century Publishing and Communications, Inc.

A Haights Cross Communications ➤ Company

http://www.chelseahouse.com

First Printing

1 3 5 7 9 8 6 4 2

Library of Congress Cataloging-in-Publication Data

Parker, Barbara Keevil.
   Miguel de Cervantes / Barbara Parker and Duane F. Parker.
      p. cm. — (The great Hispanic heritage)
Includes bibliographical references and index.
   ISBN 0-7910-7252-5
   1. Cervantes Saavedra, Miguel de, 1547–1616.—Juvenile literature. 2. Authors,
Spanish—Classical period, 1500–1700—Biography—Juvenile literature.
I. Parker, Duane F. (Duane Frank), 1937– II. Title. III. Series.
PQ6337 .P37 2003
863'.3—dc21

                                                                    2002153048

Table of Contents

1

Tilting at the Windmills:

The Imagination

Let your imagination whisk you back in time to a village in Spain, where a middle-aged man is writing in a small study.

Miguel de Cervantes leans back in his chair. His fingers ache from long hours of grasping his writing quill. He wipes his tired eyes with his right hand, then massages the numb fingers of his useless left hand. Stroking his white beard, he looks again at his manuscript. A wry smile crosses his face as he reads the chapter he just completed.

At that moment they caught sight of some thirty or forty windmills . . . as soon as Don Quixote saw them he said to his squire: "Fortune is guiding our affairs. . . . Look over there, friend Sancho Panza, where more than thirty monstrous giants appear. I intend to do battle with them and take all their lives . . ."

"What giants?" asked Sancho Panza.

"Those you see there," replied his master, "with their long arms . . ."

Windmills become monstrous giants in *Don Quixote*, Cervantes' imaginative novel about Alonso Quixano, a man who longs so desperately to become a knight that he confuses fantasy with reality, and believes that he actually is one. In his disillusionment, Alonso Quixano adopts the name Don Quixote and embarks on a journey for adventure.

"Take care, your worship," said Sancho; "those things over there are not giants but windmills, and what seem to be their arms are the sails, which are whirled around in the wind and make the millstone turn."

"It is quite clear," replied Don Quixote, "that you are not experienced in the matter of adventures . . ."

As he spoke, he dug his spurs into his steed Rocinante, paying no attention to his squire's shouted warning that beyond all doubt they were windmills and not giants he was advancing to attack. But he went on, so positive that they were giants that he neither listened to Sancho's cries nor noticed what they were, even when he got near them. Instead he went on shouting in a loud voice: "Do not fly cowards, vile creatures, for it is one knight alone who assails you."

> At that moment a slight wind arose, and the great sails began to move . . . covering himself with his shield and putting his lance in the rest, he urged Rocinante forward at a full gallop and attacked the nearest windmill, thrusting his lance into the sail. But the wind turned it with such violence that it shivered his weapon in pieces, dragging the horse and his rider with it, and sent the knight rolling badly injured across the plain.
>
> *Don Quixote, Part I*

Miguel de Cervantes knew from experience what a wonderful tool a man's imagination could be. It can cause a man to go mad, to believe what isn't true is reality, and it can save a tortured soul from the evils of prison.

Too many times in his life, Miguel de Cervantes had been a prisoner. One of these times was in 1597, when he was incarcerated based on a false accusation that he was shortchanging the government by keeping tax money he collected. Cervantes had worked for the king as a tax collector, and although it was unlikely that he was actually guilty of any wrong doing, he was jailed.

Cervantes was an injured war hero, a *hildago* (Spanish gentleman), a poet, and a good Catholic. Imprisonment was quite a blow. The cries of prisoners filled with despair, the coughing spells of the sick, the vile aromas of urine and sweat and vomit—all were indignities Cervantes undoubtedly was forced to endure. It would have been hard for anyone to cope with these conditions.

Miguel de Cervantes chose a coping strategy that would make him famous for centuries to come. During his life he journeyed from town to town, first as a child, then as a soldier, and later as a tax collector; he had met royalty, peasants, artisans, and noblemen. As a prisoner, he retreated into his imagination, pulling together characters from his life as well as characters from the books he had read. In his mind, he developed the story of a man named Alonso Quixano. Once Cervantes left prison in April 1598, he wrote it down and had it published under the title of *The Ingenious Gentleman Don Quixote de la Mancha.*

In the story, Alonso Quixano, a middle-aged man from the district of La Mancha in southern Spain, dreams of becoming a knight. He longs to wear armor, carry a sword, and ride a horse decorated with elegant blankets and trinkets. He dreams of jousting with other knights; to have the secret admiration of fair maidens; to go for months, maybe years, on a holy quest. Alonso's fantasies, like Miguel's, evolve from reading books that crammed his shelves, books with covers worn from reading and rereading, books filled with tales of knights and maidens. Swept up in the imaginary world of courtly romances, he yearns for bygone times when knights wandered from place to place in search of adventures, seeking to test their courage and uphold their honor.

Eventually Alonso becomes so obsessed with the idea of becoming a knight that he loses touch with reality and believes that he actually is a knight.

Alonso polishes his great grandfather's old, dilapidated, and rickety suit of armor and prepares to begin a quest. Fashioning a pasteboard visor for his broken helmet, naming his aging horse Rocinante, and changing his name to Don Quixote de la Mancha, he takes to the road in search of adventure.

All knights were supposed to be in love with a fair and noble lady, so Don Quixote wants to love a beautiful maiden, too. A big, strapping peasant girl named Aldonza serves well as Don Quixote's imaginary fair maiden, Dulcinea.

After a series of misadventures, Don Quixote ends up back home. His niece, his housekeeper, a priest, and a barber decide that his books caused his madness and burn them. When he recovers from his wounds, his niece tells him an evil enchanter destroyed his library.

Don Quixote refuses to allow family and friends to deter his quest. He sneaks away from his home and meets a poor workingman named Sancho Panza. Quixote talks him into becoming his squire. The two men slip out of town—Don Quixote riding his horse, Rocinante, and Sancho riding his donkey, Dapple. Windmills await them.

In Cervantes' famous novel, *Don Quixote*, the main character Don Quixote convinces a poor workingman named Sancho Panza to accompany him on his journeys. This engraving from the 1800s depicts the fictional Quixote and Panza setting out on horseback in their elusive search for glory and riches.

The cast of characters has become part and parcel of our cultural heritage the world over. Don Quixote is a foolish man who blunders into fights and loses, but doesn't learn anything from his mistakes. Sancho Panza's greediness clouds his common sense so much that he believes Don's promises of riches and rewards. Dulcinea, the girl of Don Quixote's fantasy, is just that—a fantasy. The real woman who serves as her model would never know he even exists.

Cervantes' influence on literature, language, and culture as a whole is immeasurable. With his quill he may have penned the very blueprint for the modern novel, and secured Don Quixote and himself an everlasting place in the imagination of readers young and old, male and female, and rich and poor alike.

Return again in your imagination to the little village in Spain. Satisfied with his cast of characters, Cervantes lifts his writing quill and bends over his writing table. He needs to stop, to give his body and his mind a rest. His imagination, however, drives him to write, and so with his quill, Miguel de Cervantes scratches the next chapter of Don Quixote's life, the battle with the gallant Basque.

CERVANTES' SELF-PORTRAIT

During his lifetime, no one was commissioned to paint a portrait of Miguel de Cervantes, so scholars are not certain of his appearance. However, in 1613, Cervantes used words to paint his self-portrait in the prologue of his *Exemplary Novels*:

This man you see here, with aquiline countenance, the chestnut hair, the smooth, untroubled brow, the bright eyes, the hooked yet well-proportioned nose, the silvery beard that less than a score [twenty] of years ago was golden, the big moustache, the small mouth, the teeth that are scarcely worth mentioning (there are but half a dozen of them altogether, in bad condition and very badly placed, no two of them corresponding to another pair), the body of medium height, neither tall nor short, the high complexion that is fair rather than dark, the slightly stooping shoulders, and the somewhat heavy build—this, I must tell you, is the author . . . commonly called Miguel de Cervantes Saavedra.

Road from Alcalá to Rome: Youth

Sunday nine days of the month of October in the Year of our Lord one thousand and five and forty and seven years was baptized miguel son of Rodrigo de cervantes and his wife doña leonor his godfathers juan pardo and he who baptized him the reverend serRano, priest of our Lady, attested by baltasar vazqz sexton and I who baptized him and sign my name

—**The Bachelor serRano,**
from Cervantes' Baptismal Certificate

Miguel de Cervantes was born in Alcalá de Henares in 1547 to Rodrigo de Cervantes and Doña Leonor de Cortinas. No official birth record exists to tell us the exact date, but biographers have speculated that he may have been born on September 29, Saint Michael's day, hence his name Miguel. Infant mortality during those times was high, so many parents had their babies baptized as close to birth as possible. If that is the case for Miguel, he may have been born even closer to

By the time of Cervantes' birth in the middle of the 1500s, Spain was already a mighty world power. Spain's rich history included the monarchy of King Ferdinand and Queen Isabella, who financed Christopher Columbus' expedition that led to his "discovery" of the "New World," the Americas, in 1492. Ferdinand and Isabella (depicted here in this oil painting) were also the initiators of the infamous Spanish Inquisition, a religious court that sought out and persecuted all non-Catholics in the kingdom.

his baptism. His baptismal certificate dated October 9, 1547 at the Church of Saint Mary the Great (Santa María la Mayor) by the family priest, Reverend Bachelor Serrano, is the earliest official record found of Cervantes' life.

It is hard to look at life in Spain when Miguel de Cervantes was born without knowing what happened earlier in Spanish history. Spain's King Ferdinand and Queen Isabella sent explorer Christopher Columbus on an adventure that opened the door to a new world, the Americas, in 1492. They also established the Inquisition, a religious court whose purpose was to find and persecute all those who were not Catholic. Burning religious heretics at the stake was a common practice.

In 1516, Charles I ascended the Spanish throne. In 1519, Charles received a second title, Holy Roman Emperor Charles V, when he was made the head of the states already aligned with the Church of Rome and was responsible for assuring their loyalty to the church.

Charles V sent explorers to conquer the New World in the name of Spain. Ferdinand Magellan sailed through what is now called the Strait of Magellan near the southern tip of South America in 1520, and in 1521 he discovered the Philippines. Hernando Cortés conquered the Aztecs in Mexico in 1522. Francisco Pizarro conquered the Incas in Peru in 1532. New territories added wealth, lands, and thus power to the Spanish empire. The explorers reinforced the image of the knight errant whose adventures brought them fame, wealth, and the respect of the Spanish people.

At the time of Cervantes' birth in 1547, Spain, led by Emperor Charles V, was rich, powerful, and feared by other countries. Charles V controlled not only Spain, but also most of Sardinia, Sicily, parts of North Africa, and nearly half of the Western Hemisphere. In addition, Charles was heir to the Hapsburg possessions in Germany, Austria, the Netherlands, and what is now Belgium. In 1547, Charles V led the Catholic forces to defeat the Protestant armies at Muhlberg, Germany.

On September 1, 1547, Spanish Inquisitional courts received their first printed *Index of Prohibited Books*. The index, first issued the year before at the Catholic University of Louvain, in Flanders, and now updated, listed books banned by the Catholic Church. Two years later, a new, more complete list would arrive that included the writings of Erasmus of Rotterdam and all Bibles translated from Latin into the vernacular (the language spoken by the people in a

This illustration, based on a painting by Jehan Georges Vibert, depicts two clergymen secretly enjoying forbidden books before they burn them. The *Index of Prohibited Books*, first issued in 1546, identified books banned by the Catholic Church, a list that included the writings of Erasmus of Rotterdam and all versions of the Bible not printed in Latin, the official language of the Roman Catholic Church.

given country). Erasmus was a Catholic theologian whose writings were critical of the abuses of the Catholic Church. While the church considered his writings heresy, Erasmus' liberal views influenced many of Cervantes' early teachers.

Spain's armies were triumphant. Its Merino wool was the finest in Europe. Its universities flourished. Silver and gold poured into Spain's treasury across the Atlantic from the Americas.

However, in 1547, the rich were getting richer, and the poor, poorer. The king spent money to build castles and monasteries, and to support his gigantic military. Spain's huge empire, however, was unable to support itself. The king levied taxes to pay the debt, and the burden fell mainly on the farmers, who were forced to pay by often-ruthless tax collectors. Only about 20 percent of the population had to pay taxes because the *hidalgo* class and the clergy, as well as civil servants, teachers, and students, were exempt.

Miguel de Cervantes' family claimed *hidalgo* status. A *hidalgo* was a person of noble birth who held a minor title. This status placed him above the commoner and made him exempt from the practice of imprisoning people who could not pay their debts. One had to prove eligibility for this status by obtaining a "properly executed patent (document) of nobility, duly sealed and beribboned and emblazoned with the family crest [that] proved by attestations that the candidate's family was and had been generally reputed to be gentry." For some reason, the Cervantes family did not have this document, which turned out to be rather problematical in Miguel's later life.

Over the centuries, countless legends developed about Miguel de Cervantes' ancestry. Cervantes was a common name at the time, and so many earlier biographers traced the wrong families when searching for his roots. What researchers know for sure is that his ancestors settled in the region of Spain known as Andalusia.

Miguel's great grandfather, Ruy Díaz de Cervantes, was a cloth merchant in Córdoba. Miguel's grandfather, Juan de Cervantes, graduated with a law certificate from Salamanca in the 1490s. Juan became a magistrate and lived in several locations. At age 30, he married Miguel's grandmother, Leonor de Torreblanca, the daughter of a Córdoban physician. They had four children, three sons they named Juan, Rodrigo, and Andrés and a daughter, Maria. Their second son, Rodrigo, the future father of Miguel de Cervantes, was born in Alcalá in 1509.

Juan worked for the Duke of Infantado, Diego Hurtado de

Mendoza. At some point, Don Martin de Mendoza, the illegitimate son of the duke, seduced Juan's daughter Maria.

At first, Don Martin was a generous lover and gave Maria expensive gifts. When Maria gave birth to his child, however, she did not receive the dowry he promised. Her father, Juan, sued the Mendozas for the dowry. The Mendozas retaliated by having Juan thrown in jail in Valladolid for professional corruption. He proved his innocence and obtained a release. Eventually, Maria received her dowry.

During the 1530s, Juan de Cervantes' family lived again in Alcalá. Because of Juan's status in the community, his family mingled with the wealthy, kept slaves and servants, raised horses, and wore expensive clothing. All three sons lived as glamorous young men about town. His oldest son, named after himself, Juan, married a wealthy woman. His second son, Rodrigo, Miguel de Cervantes' father, is believed to have been deaf since infancy. However, Rodrigo enjoyed success as an equestrian and amateur player of the viol, a musical instrument.

In 1538, Juan separated from his wife and left Alcalá to return to Córdoba, taking his youngest son, Andrés, with him. Juan lived out his life in Córdoba as a judge of confiscated property for the Inquisition. Although he had suffered legal entanglements during his career, he was a successful man with a comfortable income. His wife, Leonor de Torreblanca, remained in Alcalá with her two remaining sons, Rodrigo and Juan.

Rodrigo's life changed when his father left Alcalá. His older brother, Juan, died in 1540. His mother suffered financial losses. The lavish lifestyle he had known became a mere memory.

Around 1542, Rodrigo married Doña Leonor de Cortinas, the daughter of a family of rural landowners who had settled around Madrid. It seems that her family did not approve of Rodrigo as a husband because they were never present at the baptisms of their grandchildren.

Rodrigo de Cervantes and Leonor de Cortinas had five children in Alcalá. A son, Andrés (1543), died as an infant. Two daughters followed, Andrea (1544) and Luisa (1546), then two sons, Miguel (1547) and Rodrigo (1550). They lived close to the church at 2 Calle de la Imagen in a little house with few comforts.

The added responsibility of a family forced Rodrigo to find work. Unable to become a physician because of his deafness, he became a surgeon, which, in sixteenth century Spain, held about the same status as being a barber or a butcher. In other words, he probably didn't enjoy a high social status. His license allowed him to bleed, repair broken arms with splints, and apply compresses under the supervision of a physician. Rodrigo's patients were the poorer citizens of Alcalá, often victims of street brawls. Rodrigo would be poor for the rest of his life.

At the time of Miguel's birth, the town of Alcalá was a populous, busy university town. Cardinal Jiménez de Cisneros, who had held public book burnings of Arabic religious literature during the Inquisition of Ferdinand and Isabella's reign, had founded the University of Alcalá de Henares in 1508. Medicine and theology were strong subjects at the university. However, the townspeople were inclined to be more interested in the humanities and literature. The presses of Alcalá were competing with the older presses in the towns of Toledo, Burgos, Salamanca, and Seville. Bookshops brimmed with plays, poems, and courtly romances, all popular in Spain during Miguel's youth.

Around 1547, the financial resources of Rodrigo's mother, Leonor de Torreblanca, ran dry. Destitute, she came to live with his family and brought her black slave with her. Rodrigo's sister Maria and her illegitimate daughter arrived as well. Suddenly Rodrigo found himself responsible for five adults and three children. Among them was his son Miguel.

Miguel's youth remains, for the most part, a mystery.

Speculations about his whereabouts and the events in his life are only possible by following his father's travels, searching for clues.

Rodrigo de Cervantes struggled financially throughout his life and moved the family from town to town. In 1551, when Miguel was four years old, his father Rodrigo moved the family to Valladolid. They traveled 130 miles on terrible roads in a hired coach that was packed to the brim with their belongings. The journey took a week. Along the way they stayed in mediocre inns.

Valladolid was one of the most prosperous cities in Spain. Although Spain had no official capital at the time, the royal court was located there. People flocked to Valladolid to petition, sue, or strategize in the halls of chancery or the antechambers of the councils. Crowds flowed through the streets to visit skillful jewelers and luxurious shops. People from all walks of life—gentlemen, businessmen, monks, beggars, students, and slaves—filled the city. The city was also home to crooks, prostitutes, and other lowlife.

Rodrigo thought they would have a better life in Valladolid because the city would have a greater amount of wealthy clients. Rodrigo borrowed money to take care of his family and to finance his business as a surgeon, but when his loans came due the following year, he was unable to pay his debts. The authorities imprisoned him on July 2, 1552. The family's possessions— a chest, a set of sheets, and a few pieces of furniture, some clothing, a sword, a viol, a grammar book, and two medical texts—were confiscated. Rodrigo's mother salvaged what she could by putting the goods in her name.

Another child, Magdalena, was born to Miguel's family on July 22, 1552.

From prison, Rodrigo managed to produce testimonies proving he and his father had honorable professions, professions not given to commoners. However, the fact that the *hidalgo* status of the Cervantes family had not been verified by letters patent, the official document which verified *hildago* status, now became a problem. Rodrigo was in and out of prison until February.

Out of money and plagued by debt, Rodrigo loaded his family, including his mother, Leonor de Torreblanca, and his sister, Maria, into another hired carriage, and with their few possessions they returned to Alcalá in the spring of 1553.

In the autumn of the same year, Rodrigo left on a pilgrimage that took him to Córdoba to find his father Juan. Biographers do not know if his family went with him. They do know however, that Rodrigo's mother did. While at first his father was not interested in reconciliation, the tensions of their relationship eased. While Rodrigo was in Córdoba, his last son was born in 1554 and named Juan, after his grandfather.

It is possible that Miguel accompanied his father and grandmother to Córdoba. In Córdoba, Miguel would have discovered school, the theater, and the picaresque, a form of prose fiction.

Biographers believe that Alonso de Vieras, a relative of the Cervantes family, taught six-year-old Miguel to read and write. Later, Miguel may have attended the Jesuit school, Saint Catherine, established in Córdoba in 1555.

Popular at the time were allegorical plays, stories with hidden meanings used to teach moral principles. Staged at St. Catherine on special occasions by the Jesuit fathers, the children acted in plays that were attended by dignitaries and parents.

The puppet theater was popular at the time as well. It is quite possible that Miguel watched the great Lope de Rueda and his puppets when he was in Córdoba in 1556. In *The Glass Licentiate*, Cervantes recalled those "wanderers" who "stuffed all, or most, of the characters of the Old and New Testament into a sack and then sat on it to eat and drink in bar rooms and taverns."

On the fringe of society in Spain's cities lived the *pícaros*.

The name referred to thieves, beggars, vagrants, con men, unemployed soldiers, and prostitutes. Although this parasitic community had always been around, its existence remained in the shadows until it caught the attention of theologians and jurists. The theologians and jurists were concerned with the increase in numbers of people who were attracted to the free and wild life found on the streets. The debates between the theologians and jurists about what to do with the *pícaros* brought the street people a visibility and prominence no one had expected. In the middle of the sixteenth century, the *pícaros* would become the subjects of a new type of Spanish literature known as the picaresque novel, a form of prose fiction that often depicted a roguish hero.

Córdoba was one of the Spanish cities known for the picaresque. Near San Nicolas Church, the Plaza del Potro was the meeting place of this shadowy community. Whether Miguel mingled with the street people while he was in Córdoba is, of course, unknown; however, his later writing reflects a knowledge about the *pícaros* he must have acquired somewhere in his travels.

In 1556 Miguel's grandfather Juan de Cervantes died; a year later his grandmother Leonor de Torreblanca died as well. Miguel's father Rodrigo lost social standing and financial protection when they died. The next seven years in Rodrigo's and Miguel's life remains a mystery.

It is known that toward the end of 1564, Rodrigo arrived in Seville and managed rental property his brother Andrés owned. Although the rental property was in one of the wealthy parishes of the city, Rodrigo lived in a lower-class neighborhood. Researchers know that his daughter Andrea accompanied him to Seville, but are not sure about the rest of the family.

Andrea had an affair with Nicolas de Ovando, son of a magistrate of the king's council and nephew of the vicar general of Castile. Nicolas broke his promise to marry Andrea, and she received the financial payoff that was customary in those days because the birth of her daughter, Constanza de Ovando, proved that her allegations of their affair were valid.

Seville was a city of luxury and poverty. It was the most prosperous city in the Andalusian Peninsula due to the fertile farmlands surrounding it, its accessibility to the Guadalquivir River, and the monopoly it had on trade with the Indies. With 100,000 residents, and new residents moving there constantly, the real estate business was booming. However, Rodrigo did not remain employed by his brother for long. He left after two years.

Miguel was 18 when they lived in Seville. He may have attended the Jesuit school there, even though it was a somewhat elite school, and a poor property manager might not have been able to afford sending his son there. Some biographers say that Miguel began classes at the Jesuit school in Seville in 1562, possibly sent there by his uncle Andres to accompany Miguel's cousin.

Around January 1565, Rodrigo returned to Alcalá. In February, he attended the vow-taking ceremony of his daughter Luisa, who entered the Carmelite nunnery of La Concepcion. She would later become the prioress there.

The sudden death of Rodrigo's mother-in-law found him with his family in Alcalá. In a few months, he left again with his family for Madrid, the new Spanish capital of King Philip II. Philip II, who was quite religious, chose Madrid because its geographical location enabled him to easily supervise the work on El Escorial, a huge monastery and royal palace he was having built.

When Philip II moved to Madrid in 1561, the councils and offices moved with him, bringing all the courtiers, functionaries, and petitioners, as well as their families and associates. A cross-section of people from high-flying adventurers to common mobsters also arrived.

In the fall of 1566, the Cervantes family settled in Madrid. On December 2, 1566, Rodrigo signed a document granting

King Philip II made the city of Madrid Spain's new capital because of its proximity to El Escorial (seen here), the huge monastery and palace that he was having built.

power of attorney to his wife, Leonor, at the time of the settlement of her mother's estate. Fifteen days later, Leonor sold part of the estate, a vineyard located in Arganda, for 7,000 *maravedís* (an ancient Spanish gold coin). Researchers believe her inheritance helped their impoverished family.

Rodrigo may have tried to start a new business, perhaps managing an apartment house. He took a loan of 800 *ducats* (gold coins worth approximately 375 *maravedís* each at the time) from Pedro Sanchez de Córdoba. He also received loans from two Italian businessmen and Alonso Getino de Guzmán, an organizer of public entertainment in the capital. One of the Italians, Francesco Locadelo, a wealthy merchant, had come to Rodrigo for lodging. When Locadelo became ill, Rodrigo and his daughter Andrea took care of him. To show his gratitude for the care he received when he needed medical attention, Locadelo gave Andrea 300 *escudos* (a gold coin worth about 400 *maravedís*, approximately the same worth as a *ducat*) plus gifts of cloth, clothing, cushions, rugs, candlesticks, pewter plates, chairs, and writing tables. Locadelo hoped these gifts would give Andrea a dowry that would permit her to marry honorably after all.

No one knows if Miguel was aware of these transactions. When Miguel moved to Madrid with his parents at age 19, he had no career. Although he loved plays and acting, he could not become an actor because he had a speech impediment. However, Getino de Guzmán and his work had a lasting effect on Cervantes' life. In October 1566, the Infanta Catalina Micaela was born to Philip II and Elizabeth of Valois. To celebrate her birth, Getino de Guzmán planned the festivities. On the triumphal arches, he displayed medallions decorated with poetic compositions. One of these compositions was a sonnet by Miguel. Though it was not a masterpiece, the poem marked the beginning of his career as a writer.

Historians believe that Miguel studied with Juan López de Hoyos, rector of the city high school, Estudio de la Villa, in 1568. In the sixteenth century, grammar lessons included composition. In addition to listening to readings and repeating the lessons mechanically, students composed either prose or poetry on subjects assigned by the teacher.

Miguel must have been an excellent pupil, because López

SIXTEENTH-CENTURY SPANISH COINAGE

Coinage systems were not standardized in Colonial Europe. Unlike the United States today, these countries used metal coins of copper, silver, and gold that were intrinsically valuable (i.e., their worth was equal to the amount of precious or semi-precious metal they were made from). In Spain, as well as other countries, several different types of coins were used concurrently.

The *maravedi* was the most basic unit of Spanish coinage. It was minted as a gold coin in the eleventh and twelveth centuries, but by the time of Cervantes in the sixteenth century, it was being produced in copper. The terms *ducat* and *escudo* were often used interchangeably, even though their worth was not exactly the same. The *ducat* was a coin, typically of gold, that originated in Sicily but was used throughout Europe including Venice, Holland, Austria, the Netherlands and, of course, Spain. Though the value of the *ducat* varied from region to region, in sixteenth-century Spain, it was worth about 375 *maravedis*. The *escudo* (from the Latin word *scutum*, meaning shield, because it bore the king's crest on one side) was a Spanish gold coin introduced to Spain in 1523 by Charles V to replace the *ducat*. It continued to be used in Spain until the middle of the nineteenth century. The *escudo* was worth about 400 *maravedis*. The silver Spanish *real* equaled 34 *maravedis*.

It's impossible to give present-day equivalents for old coins because of the rate of inflation in Spain in the sixteenth century and today. The best estimation of the value of the *ducat/escudo* during Cervantes' time would be about US$10 today. Based on these coin values and our current-day prices, Cervantes would have received about $1,500 for the first part of Don Quixote. Bookstores would have sold it for $20.

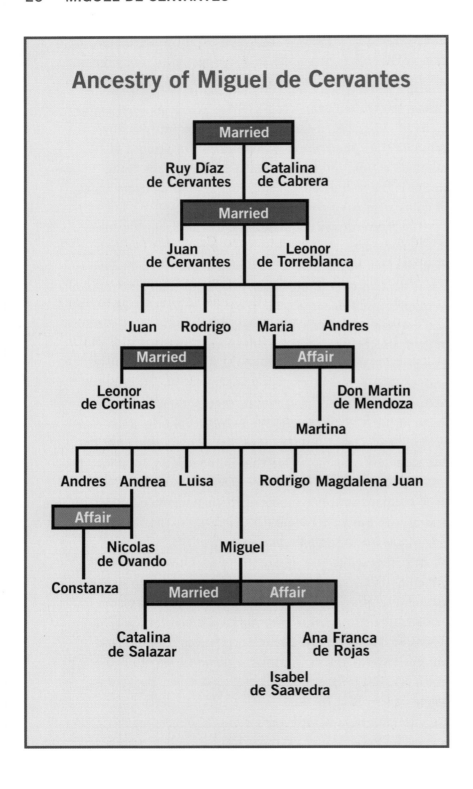

Ancestry of Miguel de Cervantes

de Hoyos requested Miguel to write four poems when Philip II's queen, Elizabeth of Valois, died at the age of 23 giving birth to another child, this one stillborn, in 1568. These words are from one of the four poems Miguel wrote:

> When war left our Hispanic soil free,
> The fairest flower on earth, with sudden flight
> Was transplanted up to heaven.

López de Hoyos included the four poems in his book, *Relacion,* with a note referring to Cervantes as his "well-beloved pupil."

Although Cervantes was developing a circle of friends with other Spanish poets at about this time, his life seems to have taken a mysterious turn. In October 1568, Miguel de Cervantes was still in Madrid writing his elegy on the queen's death. Just one year later, in December 1569, three months after the publication of the *Relacion,* Cervantes was settled in Rome. It is unclear what caused him to move to Rome and abandon the life as a writer he seemed to have started.

3

The Fighter at Lepanto:
Military Years

To the war I am driven by necessity.
If I had money, forsooth I would not go.

—Cervantes, *Don Quixote*

In December 1569, Cervantes was settled in Rome. Although it is
not clear why he traveled to Rome, the following may provide a clue.

In Madrid on September 15, 1569, agents of the king issued a
royal warrant ordering the arrest of a student named Miguel de
Cervantes for wounding a master mason, Antonio de Sigura, in a
duel. Supposedly the incident took place under the colonnade
of the royal palace. The common sentence for anyone drawing
a weapon near royalty or royal quarters was chopping off the
offender's right hand at the wrist and exiling him for 10 years.
However, the accused, Miguel de Cervantes, had left the area before
the sentence could be imposed.

Although the name and dates match, there is a question about

Scholars still speculate about what compelled Cervantes to leave his homeland of Spain for Italy. Possibly Cervantes fled Spain as an outlaw, escaping both exile and potential dismemberment for his involvement in a duel near royal quarters. Another theory suggests that Cervantes left simply to achieve success as a chief officer to a Vatican official. This engraving of Cervantes was made in the 1700s, long after his death.

how and why the son of a surgeon would have been in such a situation. Cervantes, when he became an author, wrote of a similar incident three times: *The Little Gypsy Girl*, where a young man and his friend kill two rivals in a duel and flee to Italy; *The Gallant Spaniard*, where the heroine tells how a suitor of hers wounds her brother in a duel, then flees to Italy; and *The Labors of Persiles and Sigismunda*, a story in which two characters travel from Spain to Italy. One story involves a soldier named Saavedra, which was a family name that Cervantes later assumed. This may indicate that he was writing about himself, and that he indeed had to leave Madrid to escape the law.

In Spain there was a common saying that there were "three roads to success: the church, the sea [that is, the New World], and the king's service."

However, if a young person had ambition, and did not choose any of these three vocations, he could attach himself to the household of some minister or diplomat. Miguel chose this fourth road to success: namely, service in the household of a diplomat in the Vatican.

In 1568, Monsignor Julio Acquaviva arrived in Madrid. Pope Pius V had sent Acquaviva to express condolences to King Philip II over the death of Don Carlos, the king's son by his first wife, Maria of Portugal (she died during labor). Acquaviva was also sent to discuss some delicate matters regarding differences between the ecclesiastical jurisdiction and the king's ministers in Milan, Naples, and Sicily. However, when Acquaviva arrived, the king's third wife, Queen Elizabeth of Valois, had died giving birth to a stillborn child. The king was not interested in talking about Don Carlos or matters concerning jurisdiction. Perhaps Acquaviva, having time on his hands, sought the company of poets. Learning of the talented Miguel de Cervantes, Acquaviva may have invited him to return to Italy as his chamberlain.

Cervantes was 21 when he arrived in Italy. There he experienced a new freedom from his family's hardships. He was probably bursting with life, enjoying himself to the fullest, as can be deduced from his novel, *The Glass Licentiate*, in which he recalls his time in Italy. He loved "the country festivals of Palermo, the abundance of Milan, the feats of Lombardy, the splendid meals of the inns . . . the free life . . . the liberty of Italy!"

His first stop in Italy was Milan. Historians describe Milan as a lighthearted place where both young and old enjoyed life and laughter and country outings. In Spain people expressed love through languishing (pining away, suffering) and sighing. In Italy he experienced a joyful language of love that influenced his later writings.

At the same time, the forges of Milan, where military armor and weapons were produced and sold throughout the world, was a reminder of crueler things to come—war.

Cervantes then traveled through the marble mountains of Carrara to Lucca. This small city welcomed Spaniards who often stayed for a short time on their way to Rome. The city offered a glimpse of the ancient grandeur of Rome with its impressive amphitheater lined with marble seats all crumbling from the forces of time. He wrote in Book IV of *Persiles*, "Now the breezes of Rome blow in our faces, now the hopes which sustain us glow in our souls, now, now I realize that I find myself possessed of what I have longed for."

Cervantes' experience in this great city seems to have inspired the eulogy of Rome that appears in his work *The Glass Licentiate*:

He visited its temples, worshiped its saintly relics and admired its grandeur; and as through the claws of the lion one comes to know its power and savage cruelty, that of Rome is revealed by its broken marbles, whole and half statues, broken arches and ruined baths, by its magnificent porticos and great amphitheaters, by its famous holy river that always fills its verges with water and beatifies (beautifies) them with the many relics of the martyrs buried on its banks, by its bridges which seem to mirror each other, and by its streets whose names alone claim authority over those of all the other cities of the world: the Via Appia, the Flaminia, the Julia, with others of the same quality. He was no less full of admiration at the arrangement of the hills: The Caelian, the Quirinal and the Vatican, with the other

En route to Rome, Cervantes traveled through the majestic, marbled mountains of Carrara to the small city of Lucca, Italy. In these small mountainside havens, Cervantes found an intimate and welcoming atmosphere before experiencing the overwhelming grandeur of Rome.

four whose names attest the greatness and majesty of Rome. He also noted the authority of the College of Cardinals, the dignity of the Supreme Pontiff, the crowds of varied people and nations. All this he gazed at, noted and stored in the back of his mind.

The retinue (followers) of Acquaviva entered the Vatican. In December 1569, Cervantes became a chamberlain for the

23-year-old prelate-diplomat, Monsignor Guilio de Acquaviva who lived and worked in the Vatican and would soon become a cardinal.

Although Cervantes had entered the prelate's service, he was required to obtain a purity-of-birth certificate verifying that he was not born out of wedlock and that there were no Moors, Jews, or converts in his bloodline. Three individuals with well-known reputations verified the certificate. One was Alonso Getino de Guzmán, the former actor and organizer of public entertainment who had become an officer of the law in Madrid. The other two were Pirro Bocchi and Francesco Musacchi, friends of Cervantes' father. Both were respected businessmen. The Bocchis were a well-known and respected family of bankers in Rome, and their recommendation would have been highly regarded in the Vatican. Miguel assumed his duties around February 1570. In May, Acquaviva was promoted to cardinal.

There is disagreement about Cervantes' role as chamberlain, since there was a hierarchy of roles chamberlains played for their lords. Some chamberlains served as "secretar[ies], major-domo[s] (people in charge of others), [and] confidants." Other chamberlains were to maintain their lords' chambers and always be ready to attend to their lords, especially when their lords went to and awoke from sleep. They were also expected to always be present at their lords' lying down and rising up, with clothes ready, and to keep their lords' shirts and linens clean, sprinkling them with musk, if necessary. Regardless of the duties, the chamberlains were to be truthful, respectful of their lords' privacy, and revere their lords. The lords might engage the chamberlains in light humor and conversation, but the distinction between who was a lord and who was a servant was clear.

While serving Acquaviva, Cervantes saw the Vatican from the inside out. He knew the servants' quarter as well as the chamber of Acquaviva.

After 15 months, Cervantes decided to leave the Vatican. Spain was engaged in war with the Turks who were assaulting the shores of the Mediterranean in the name of the Ottoman Empire. Cervantes left Rome, shedding the robes of a chamberlain for the bright colors and plumes of the military. The actual dates when Cervantes joined the military are contradictory. His name doesn't appear on Philip II's army payroll until 1572. Later, however, the purity-of-blood inquiries held during his captivity in Algiers and on his return suggest he was a soldier as early as 1568. A witness at a 1578 investigation testified that Cervantes claimed to have been in the military for two years at the time of the Battle of Lepanto. In that case, he would have enlisted in August or September 1570 at the Spanish military depot in Rome.

Cervantes enlisted in the army led by Don Miguel de Moncada. Officials promoted Moncada to *maesre de campo* (field commander) after his leadership in the war in Granada. Moncada was viewed as a noble gentleman, who was brave and displayed sound judgment. He had served the king since youth and continued his service into old age. Moncada commanded about 3,000 men, organized into 10 companies called a *tercio* or brigade. Each company consisted of about 250 men led by a captain.

Cervantes' captain was Don Diego de Urbina. Urbina came from Guadalajara, a city near Alcalá, Cervantes' birthplace. Captain Diego de Urbina noticed the spirited man from a neighboring town and most likely considered him with affection as a fellow countryman.

Those enlisted in military service came from backgrounds quite different from Cervantes, who had studied in school and served in the Vatican. Most enlisted men were a strange mixture of poor farm boys fleeing starvation, hoodlums from the slums, disinherited sons of noblemen, students who had run out of money, and poets out to see what life was like.

Most armies at the time were corrupt. Officers took bribes for various reasons, while paymasters withheld money from soldiers' pay. Pay was often late and so the soldiers would engage in armed robbery, attacks on citizens, begging, and other unruly behavior to obtain food and other necessities.

Historians have wondered why Cervantes enlisted in the military, since he had enjoyed life in Rome. Although his experience in the Vatican may have been less than exciting, it was a total change in direction to enlist in military service. It is possible that he joined the military out of loyalty to his country and to earn a living.

While in the army, Cervantes traveled around Italy. He later wrote of Venice, "its riches were infinite, its government prudent, its site impregnable, its opulence great, its surroundings pleasant, and finally, all of it, in itself and in its every part worthy of a fame which reaches all parts of the terrestrial globe." In Venice he was undoubtedly influenced by the sensation of light and color captured in paintings from local artists. He visited the religious houses, sacred relics, and monuments. His time in Venice made a lasting impression on him, which affected his later writings.

In the bustling city of Naples, Cervantes seems to have met and fallen in love with a beautiful young woman. Scholars look to his first novel, *La Galatea*, where he speaks of a woman he called Silena. From this relationship it appears that a son, Promontorio, was born out of wedlock. Later in life, Cervantes wrote about a son in a poem:

> . . . He called me 'father', and I called him 'son' . . .
> . . . Said Promontorio: 'Tell me if I'm right
> That some misfortune, father, brings thee here . . .

No record exists of Silena or if that was her real name.

While Cervantes most likely spent his early time in the army traveling and gaining worldly experience, the world around him was preparing for war. The constant battle cry was "The Turks are on us! The Turks are on us!" War preparations increased and Cervantes, like others, undoubtedly caught the spirit of "heroic impatience" for battle.

Cervantes left no record of his military service, so biographers created the historical record from knowledge about the conflicts between the Ottoman Turks and the European Christians, and records about specific battles.

When Cervantes joined the service, the Ottoman Turks had been expanding their influence by capturing territories and cities formerly held by Christians. The struggle between Christian Europe and the Ottoman Turks had been occurring for 50 years.

THE OTTOMAN TURKS

In the seventh century, a man named Muhammad ibn Abd Allah became the founder of Islam in the city of Mecca (in present day Saudi Arabia). When he was about 40 years old, Muhammad was visited by the angel Gabriel, who told Muhammad that he had been chosen to be God's messenger. Over a period of the next 23 years, the angel continued to visit Muhammad with revelations from God. Gabriel taught Muhammad in verses, which Muhammad immediately wrote down. These verses include the revelation that there is only one god (a belief called monotheism), Allah, and that Muhammad was the last prophet in a line of prophets that includes Moses and Jesus of Nazareth. These revelations are now compiled into the *Qur'an*, the Islamic holy book, and are Allah's exact words.

Muhammad developed a following, and he encouraged his followers to increase their influence by converting others to Islam after his death. The Islamic religion grew in size from its base in Arabia through North Africa and into Eastern Europe. By 1553 the Muslim Turks, who viewed non-Muslims as infidels, were at the doorstep of Vienna. By 1570, the Christian nations were fearful that the Sultan Selim II, head of the Ottoman (Turkish) Empire, would attack and overrun the Christian nations, including Spain and Italy. It was in battling the invading Ottoman Turks at the Battle of Lepanto that Cervantes' left hand was wounded.

The Ottoman Empire reached from southern Russia to the Gulf of Aden and from Baghdad to the beaches of Morocco. Constantinople, its capital, had a larger population than Spain's 10 biggest cities combined. The Ottoman Turks weren't strong enough to defeat the western countries. Instead, their Barbary pirates from North Africa raided western ships and attacked the coasts of Italy and Spain.

The Vatican was very troubled by the movements of the Ottoman Turks, and proposed that the western countries form an alliance. Spain joined the Vatican in this alliance. While the pope wanted the Venetians to join the alliance, the Venetians resisted, because they did considerable business with the Turks and wanted to keep peace with them. They hoped to protect their access to Asia Minor, the North Sea, and the East.

In July 1570, the Turks invaded Cyprus, the farthest outpost of the Venetian territory, making it clear that they were not interested in peace. By the end of September, the Venetians began talks with the pope and Philip II. A first attempt to rescue Cyprus ended in defeat. On May 20, 1571, Venice agreed to the establishment of the Holy League by signing a three-year pact with its allies. Together they prepared for war against the Turks and began assembling an armada. Don Juan de Austria became the commander.

Don Juan arrived in Genoa on June 27, 1571. He headed 47 galleys that included the *tercios* of Don Lope de Figueroa and Don Miguel de Moncada. Moncada had added two companies to his *tercio* in Naples. Cervantes, as well as his brother Rodrigo, were among the recruits.

In August of 1571, the Spanish squadron moved to Messina to be joined by the papal and the Venetian fleets. The combined fleet of more than 300 vessels with 80,000 men aboard was impressive. All ships were to be in perfect shape before sailing. The Spanish fleet arrived in excellent condition, but the Venetian fleet did not, partly because of recent battles. Also, the Venetian troops were considered less than top quality. Don Juan worked hard to get the ships and crews ready for battle. War preparations were completed and, after waiting out a storm, the fleet set sail from Messina on September 16. The combined fleets—the Venetians, the Spaniards, and the papal troops—were divided into three combat armadas, plus a scouting force and one in reserve. Cervantes sailed on the *Marquesa* commanded by an Italian, Francisco de Santo Pietro.

On board the *Marquesa,* Cervantes was with war heroes whom he admired at first. His view seems to have changed as he heard them grumble about their way of life, watched them cheat at card games, engage in drunkenness, and act crude and cruel.

Another troubling part of life at sea was the harsh way the oarsmen were treated. The oarsmen were a mixture of convicts and slaves. A boatswain ruled the oarsmen and walked up and down the ship making sure their rowing was keeping pace. The boatswain carried a whip and used it to enforce discipline. If a slave was rebellious, the boatswain would order the slave to be hung up by his wrists and beaten with a whip. After this punishment, he would be cut down and his sores would be rubbed with salt and vinegar to increase the pain. Then the oarsman would be sent back to continue rowing. The punishment would stop short of death. If the rower died, the boatswain had to pay the boat owner the price of the slave. It was a cruel and very hard life. Later in his writings, Cervantes included stories about the slaves and the boatswains.

The Holy League's armada sailed to the Island of Corfu, arriving on September 27, 1571, to make final preparations for their assault against the Turks. In the meantime, Cervantes became very ill. Delirious and shaking with fever from malaria, he ended up on a ship infested with vermin in a space below the decks. He was "seasick, suffocated, eaten by fleas and lice, disgusted by the grossness of the crew and the slaves of the row galley." During the night he would fight off the rats that ran freely on the ship.

The *Marquesa* was fast and streamlined for its day. It was at least 130 feet long and about 16 feet wide. The *Marquesa* was a narrow vessel with two castles fore and aft, two masts and a mainsail, and probably 30 or 40 banks of oars. Around 400 individuals were crammed aboard the ship, including 200 rowers, 30 sailors responsible for navigation and upkeep, and about 200 soldiers ready for battle.

Ship battles involved various military actions including ramming enemy ships, firing guns at close range, throwing spears from one ship toward another, burnings, and any action that would sink or disable the opponent's ship and crew. The ships would approach each other, the infantry would hook them together with grappling irons, and then the soldiers would jump on board and fight hand-to-hand.

On October 7, 1571, the combined fleet approached the narrow channel of Lepanto, Greece. They sighted the masts of the Turkish fleet about 15 miles away, moving through the channel. The Christian galley gangs brought their ships into a line facing the Turks. As the two fleets prepared for battle, Don Juan boarded a small frigate (boat) and raced from ship to ship, warning the troops not to panic and to have courage. He promised freedom to the galley slaves if there was victory.

The Turks formed an irregular line opposite the Christians. When the two fleets drew closer, the Spanish galleons opened fire. Two Turkish warships were sunk.

At midday, the cannons from Cervantes' ship fired their first broadside. Cervantes, who was alone and very ill, heard the cries of the troops, "to arms, to arms." The attack had started. Cervantes flung aside his blanket, grabbed his armor and his harquebus (gun) and went on deck to engage in the attack. He asked the captain for an assignment, but when the captain saw his shaky legs and yellowed face, he told him that he was too ill and should go back below the deck. Cervantes refused. It is recorded that he said:

Gentlemen . . . on every occasion when His Majesty has been at war up to now and I have been sent to it. I have served as a good soldier, and thus today I will not do less though I am ill and fevered; it is better to fight and die in the service of God and His Majesty than to go below. Señor Captain, put me in the most dangerous place and there I will take my stand and die fighting.

The captain was reluctant, but assigned Cervantes to a post with 12 other men. In this post, Cervantes could see the battle unfold before his eyes.

The Turkish fleet and the Christian fleet engaged in fierce battle. Opposing galleys tried to ram each other, smashing oars. Grappling hooks locked the Spanish galleons to the Turkish galleons. The infantrymen from both sides swarmed toward each other to slaughter as many men as possible with the goal of capturing the ship. Cervantes stood on the *Marquesa* loading and firing his harquebus. Two shots fired by the Turks hit Cervantes' chest. Another bullet seriously wounded his left hand. He fell to the deck and lost consciousness. However, he later wrote that in spite of his personal injuries, "my happiness was so great, to see the rude infidel defeated by the Christians, that it pervaded my soul."

Historians have called the Battle of Lepanto one of the most severe military battles in history. Throughout his life, Cervantes would refer to his participation in this battle as a high point of his life. Officers recognized Cervantes as a hero for his outstanding service while very ill and for his sacrifice in battle. He eventually even received extra pay for his participation in the Battle of Lepanto. Cervantes considered the military as the highest profession and most honorable human service.

His ship returned to Messina where he was hospitalized for six months, from October 31, 1571 until the end of April 1572. Hospitals at the time were over-crowded and lacked privacy, sanitary conditions were poor, and treatments were

The great naval Battle of Lepanto, fought at the mouth of the Gulf of Patras, Greece, marked the end of Turkish naval supremacy, and, arguably, the decline of the Ottoman Empire. Cervantes' heroic determination to fight in the battle, despite being ill, distinguished him as a soldier and resulted in the maiming of his left hand.

primitive compared to modern standards. Cervantes' wounded left hand became gangrenous and he was at risk of losing it. A physician was called to treat his hand. Although he had incurred permanent damage, the painful procedure enabled Cervantes to keep his hand.

Cervantes left the hospital on April 24, 1572, and returned

to military service with a new title, elite trooper, and increased pay for his previous heroic service. In the winter of 1572, Cervantes traveled to Naples, where he rejoined his brother, Rodrigo, whom he had not seen since the Battle of Lepanto.

Cervantes participated in several battles against the Ottoman Turks during this time. In April 1573, as the Holy League troops were preparing for what they hoped would be a final battle against the Turks, the Venetians signed a treaty with the Turks, giving up Cyprus. The other members of the alliance were angry at news of the treaty. The Spaniards considered it treason. Apparently, the Venetian leadership had decided to sign the treaty due to commercial interests and fear that the Turks would defeat the alliance.

Meanwhile, another major problem developed. Barbary pirates were increasing the number of raids on the coasts of Spain and Italy. Slave prisons in North Africa were filling up with Christian captives. Stopping the corsairs (pirates) was not effective due to the cost of maintaining a permanent fleet in the area and the difficulty in recruiting rowers. So, instead of battling the pirates, they decided to seize the pirates' dens. The question was which one to seize, Tunis or Algiers in North Africa. Spanish military leaders discussed the benefits of each location, and finally King Philip II decided to capture Tunis. On October 8, 1573, the second anniversary of Lepanto, the Spanish landed at Tunis and took over the fort. Cervantes fought in this battle. Afterward, he traveled with the fleet to several different ports including the Italian ports of Naples and Genoa. Meanwhile the Turks retook Tunis.

Cervantes received troubling news from home. His family continued to have financial problems. Cervantes, lacking financial resources himself, decided to return to his homeland, Spain, where he hoped the government would name him a captain and place him in charge of a new company that would return to Italy. It was a long shot because such positions were usually given to soldiers with at least 10 years of service and without damaged hands.

Cervantes requested letters of recommendation from his military superiors in Italy, Don Juan and the Duke of Sessa, and hoped this would show he was worthy of appointment as captain. With letters in hand, Cervantes left Italy during the early part of September 1575 on the ship *El Sol*. It was one of four vessels sailing for Barcelona. A fierce storm pushed the *El Sol* away from the protection of the other ships. After the storm ended, the other Spanish ships were nowhere to be seen.

Different ships were approaching. Barbary pirates were closing in on the *El Sol*. Although the Spaniards tried to defend themselves, they were far outnumbered by the pirates. With no other choice, the Spanish surrendered. The pirates tied their prisoners and threw them on the deck of the pirates' vessel. With their captives, the pirates set sail for Algiers. A new chapter was about to begin in Cervantes' life.

4

Captive in Algiers:

Five Years in Prison

When I arrived, a captive, and saw this land,
Ill-famed in all the world, whose bosom conceals,
Protects, embraces such a throng of pirates,
I could not keep from weeping.

—Cervantes, *Life in Algiers*

It was September 3, 1575, when Arnaut Mami, the head of three
Barbary ships, along with his lieutenant, Dali Mami, swarmed
the *El Sol*, killing crewmembers and plundering the ship. Miguel
and Rodrigo de Cervantes were among the prisoners. Twenty-eight-
year-old Miguel walked from the pirate ship in chains.

Once the pirates reached Algiers, they divided the plunder. It
was Cervantes' fate to become the captive of Dali Mami. The letters
of recommendation for his military service that he carried from Don
Juan and the Duke of Sessa made the pirate think his captive was an
important person. As a result, Dali Mami demanded a high ransom

44

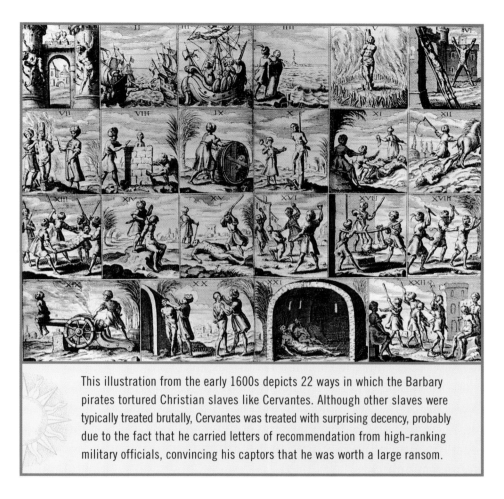

This illustration from the early 1600s depicts 22 ways in which the Barbary pirates tortured Christian slaves like Cervantes. Although other slaves were typically treated brutally, Cervantes was treated with surprising decency, probably due to the fact that he carried letters of recommendation from high-ranking military officials, convincing his captors that he was worth a large ransom.

of 500 gold *escudos,* an amount the poor Cervantes family couldn't afford.

Algiers was the leading port of North Africa and the main base of the Barbary pirates. Cervantes was amazed when he arrived. The port hummed with activity and provided shelter and supplies for ships from many different countries. The city, crowded with more than 12,000 houses, was home to 150,000 people, a mixture of Turks, Moors, and Jews. Algiers had over 100 mosques, many public baths with hot and cold running water, and a good hospital. Its markets were one of the main trading centers of the Mediterranean.

Algiers was also the hub of the Christian slave market. At the time that Cervantes arrived, about 25,000 Christian slaves were living there. Their captors kept them chained in the state prisons. Those who were not likely to be ransomed were put to work on galleys, in private households, or around the city, doing maintenance work such as sweeping, wood-cutting, building, and tending the orchards and gardens surrounding the city. Galley slaves wore chains only during their three- or four-months-a-year period on the boats, not the working slaves. Cervantes' captor, however, kept him in chains and forced him to find his own food.

Cervantes was locked in a prison called a *bano,* where Christian captives belonging to the king, as well as private individuals, were kept until their ransoms arrived. If their ransoms did not arrive, the Turks made them work, hoping this would force them to write more urgently for their ransoms.

Cervantes' ransom did not arrive. His chores as a prisoner included going into the streets to fetch water and other supplies. As he walked the streets, the people called him nasty names and children made fun of him and threw stones at him because he was a Christian. He had to beg for the little food that he ate.

Miguel de Cervantes expressed his personal feelings about his captivity in his book, *Life in Algiers*:

> I, however, was one of those held for ransom, for when it was discovered that I was a captain, although I declared my scanty means and lack of fortune, nothing could dissuade them from including me among the gentlemen and those waiting to be ransomed. They put a chain on me, more as a mark of this than to keep me safe, and so I spent my life in that *bano* with several other gentlemen and persons of quality marked out as held for ransom. Though at times, or rather almost always, we suffered from hunger and scanty clothing, nothing distressed us so much as hearing

and seeing at every turn the unexampled and unheard-of cruelties my master inflicted upon the Christians. Every day he hanged a man, impaled one, cut off the ears of another, and all with so little provocation, or so entirely without any, that the Turks acknowledged he did it for its own sake and because he was by nature murderously disposed toward the whole human race.

Captives held for ransom must have felt like chunks of meat as their owners tried to sell them. However, the captives did have one source of support from monks, mainly of the Trinitarian and Mercedarian religious orders, who negotiated for prisoner releases.

Cervantes wanted to leave Algiers as soon as possible. As a ransomed slave he had little to do except brood about his captivity, watch the sufferings of captives not as fortunate as he, and dream of freedom. He thought of notifying his relatives of his imprisonment by sending a message with ransomed captives returning to Spain, but knowing his family's financial problems, he knew they could not pay the ransom. His only route to freedom was to escape.

FIRST ESCAPE ATTEMPT

Around January 1576, he began to plan an escape. A Moor agreed to lead him and other Christian captives to Orán. Orán was a city held by the Spanish, but it was 200 miles away. After the Moor led them out of Algiers, he deserted Cervantes and the captives. Without their guide, they would perish on their own; it became necessary for them to return to Algiers. Cervantes wrote of this difficult time in his work *A Captive's Tale*:

> Now hunger afflicts me
>   and thirst torments me;
>   now my strength fails me
>   and my only hope of escaping
>   this agony is to give myself up

to whoever will capture me again.

Now I have lost my sense of direction;
I know not what is the way to Orán . . .

Their only choice was to turn back. When they returned to Algiers, Cervantes took all responsibility for the escape attempt.

Most recaptured fugitives received atrocious punishments; however, Miguel and two of his companions received only minor punishment. Miguel's master probably spared him because he was expecting to get a large ransom for him. The two companions were ransomed around March. When they returned to Spain, they may have served as messengers to Miguel and Rodrigo's family.

In April 1576 and again in February 1577, Cervantes' father tried without luck to get Pedro de Córdoba to pay him the 800 *ducats* Pedro had borrowed 10 years earlier. His father also sold family goods and presented several petitions in an attempt to raise money for the release of his sons. His appeals for financial aid were unsuccessful.

Doña Leonor, Cervantes' mother, tried to raise money. She dressed as a grieving widow (although her husband was alive) and approached the Council of the Crusade for the ransom funds. On December 16, 1576, she received a loan of 60 *ducats* for the ransom of her two sons. She gave the money to the Mercedarian friars who were leaving for Algiers to negotiate the release of as many captives as they could afford.

The Mercedarians, a Spanish religious order, sent three monks to redeem captives. When they arrived in Algiers, Dali Mami's ransom of 500 *ducats* for Miguel was more than they could afford. Miguel convinced the monks to buy his brother Rodrigo's freedom instead of his. The pasha, Rodrigo's master, received 300 *ducats* from the monks and released Rodrigo. In August, Rodrigo and around 100 prisoners left Algiers for their homeland, Spain.

SECOND ESCAPE ATTEMPT

Miguel made plans for a second escape, an escape he had planned even before his brother left. When Rodrigo returned to Spain, he was to arrange for a frigate to come to the Barbary Coast during the night to rescue Christian captives. Early in May, Dali Mami was away. Miguel chose this time to begin leading 14 Christian captives out of the city to a cave hidden in a garden three miles east of Algiers. Each night Miguel led one captive to the cave. With the help of a gardener, a slave named Juan, the 14 captives spent up to five months hidden in the cave. Miguel arranged for their food and encouraged them as they waited for the frigate to arrive. Miguel joined them eight days before the frigate was due to arrive.

On the night of September 28, 1577, the frigate appeared offshore at the time arranged. The prisoners waited on shore for the sailors to come for them. However, the sailors didn't come. Something caused the sailors to panic and they left. Two nights later, the frigate returned to retrieve the waiting prisoners, but one of the prisoners betrayed the others. The Turks recaptured them on the morning of September 30.

Chained and manacled, the guards took Cervantes before Hassan Veneziano, the governor-general, or king. Subjects of Hassan were in awe of his reputation as a brutal man. When Hassan ordered Cervantes to tell who had helped him with the escape plan, Cervantes declared he was the only one responsible for the attempted escape. He refused to name anyone else. Usually Hassan's punishment for such a crime would be to inflict beatings and torture including disfigurement or dismemberment. Cervantes, however, just landed in the king's prison for five months, an unusually light sentence. Historians do not known why his sentence was so light. Unfortunately, one person did suffer a cruel punishment. On October 3, Hassan's executioners hung the gardener, who had assisted Cervantes with the escape plan, by one foot until he died.

THIRD ESCAPE ATTEMPT

Miguel was not idle during those five months in prison. He sent a Moor to Orán with a letter to the Spanish governor-general there, Don Martín de Córdoba, who was the commander of Orán and its forces and who had once been a captive of the Muslims. He wanted Córdoba to return with the Moor to Algiers to help him escape along with three other men who were confined by the king.

Unfortunately, the Moor carrying the message was caught near Orán. When his captors found the letter he carried, they look him back to Hassan Pasha in Algiers. When Hassan saw the signature of Miguel de Cervantes on the letters, he had the Moor impaled and sentenced Cervantes to 2,000 blows. That many hits meant certain death, but they were never inflicted. Historians are not clear why Hassan spared Cervantes, but perhaps Dali Mami or some other unknown patron intervened.

In Spain, Cervantes' family continued to try to help him. In March 1578, Rodrigo presented another request for money to the Council of Castile, but it was rejected again. His mother and his sisters also tried to raise money for his release. In July, Cervantes' mother asked the Council of War for permission to export merchandise to Algiers. Because

AGI MORATO

Agi Morato was the Grand Turk's emissary. In March 1573, and again in August 1577, Morato made the first secret overtures to Spain that eventually led to the Constantinople negotiations, in which Spain and the Turks formed the Hispano-Turkish truce of 1579–81.

In Algiers, Morato may have summoned Cervantes to help plan the secret meetings with King Philip II. If this is true, Cervantes' contact with such a high-placed official might explain why he was pardoned twice by Hassan.

she had an affidavit from the Duke of Sessa, the king gave her a license to spend 2,000 *ducats* to ransom Cervantes. However, she was unable to get financial backing and had not yet repaid the earlier advance of 60 *ducats* from the Council.

On October 1,1578, Don Juan of Austria died of typhus. Two months later, in December, the Duke of Sessa also died. When word of their deaths reached Cervantes in Algiers, he mourned the loss of his hero, Don Juan, and his supporter, the Duke of Sessa.

During Cervantes' imprisonment, he met many of the Christian slaves. His reputation as a person who took a special interest in others, and as one who would not betray his friends, was known among the captives as well as his captors.

FOURTH ESCAPE ATTEMPT

Cervantes' fourth attempt to escape came in September 1579. Cervantes met a Spanish renegade, Licentiate Giron, an Andalusian in Algiers. Giron was a free citizen in Algiers because he had converted to the Muslim faith. Now Giron wanted to return to Spain. Cervantes convinced Giron to outfit a local frigate and then use it to return 60 captives to Spain. Giron received financial backing from a Valencian businessman, Onofre Exarque, who pledged 1,300 *doubloons* (one *doubloon* equaled approximately eight *escudos* or *ducats*) for the purchase of the ship. Cervantes chose 60 fellow captives who agreed to reimburse Onofre. The 60 captives, including Cervantes, were ready to leave in early October.

A renegade named Cayban went to Hassan and told him of the plan. However, the real person responsible for the defeat of the plan was Dr. Juan Blanco de Paz, an unfrocked Dominican friar from Salamanca, who had sent Cayban to Hassan. Why Juan Blanco hated Cervantes enough to betray him is unknown. Perhaps Cervantes had not included him on the list of 60 people to escape. Perhaps Juan Blanco resented Cervantes' popularity with the prisoners.

Onofre, afraid Cervantes would implicate him, offered to ransom Cervantes with his own money and send him back to Spain. Miguel refused the offer and said he would never tell who was involved. Cervantes surrendered, and once again appeared before Hassan to assume full responsibility. Hassan told Cervantes he would hang him if he didn't name the others, but Cervantes remained silent. For five months Cervantes was kept prisoner in the king's palace.

It was during Cervantes' imprisonment that Dali Mami returned to Algiers. Dali Mami agreed to sell Cervantes to Hassan Pasha for 500 *escudos*. Six months later Hassan would raise his ransom to 1000 *escudos*.

In Spain, Cervantes' mother succeeded in getting a delay for the repayment of the 60 *ducats* she previously borrowed. She was also able to get the remaining 30-odd *ducats*, originally given to the Mercedarian friars for Rodrigo and Miguel, transferred to the Trinitarian friars who were planning a trip to Algiers. On July 31, 1579, Cervantes' mother, still posing as a widow, gave 250 *ducats* to the two friars, Juan Gil and Antonio de la Bella, for the ransom of Cervantes, "who is 33 years old, crippled in his left hand, and has a blond beard." They would be the negotiators. Andrea, Miguel's sister, contributed another 50 *ducats*. The Cervantes family hoped the Catholic order would provide any extra amount needed to pay the ransom. In September, the Crusade council contributed 475 *ducats* toward the expedition. The friars sailed for Algiers the following May.

By August 3, 1580, the friars had ransomed 108 prisoners who had set sail that day for Valencia, accompanied by Antonio de la Bella. Cervantes was not among them. Juan Gil stayed in Algiers to continue bargaining. Between August 8 and September 8, he succeeded in buying freedom for seven more prisoners. With money from so many sources, the friars tried to use the money to obtain the most releases. Juan Gil carried 300 *ducats* designated for Cervantes, but now the asking price was 1,000.

This woodcut, dating to Cervantes' time, depicts monks paying Muslims like the Barbary pirates for the release of Christian prisoners. The Trinitarian monk Juan Gil was part of a team of people, including the Council of the Crusade and members of Cervantes' family, who compiled funds to pay the high ransom set for Cervantes' release. After five years of captivity in the North African city of Algiers, Miguel de Cervantes was finally freed.

Hassan, whose term in office was ending, planned to leave Algiers for Constantinople and to take all of his slaves with him. Juan Gil continued to bargain with Hassan. Finally, Hassan told the friar he would let him choose any of his captives and slaves for 500 *ducats* a head.

On September 19, 1580, Hassan's men took Cervantes on board ship along with Hassan's other slaves and chained them to the benches of his galley before the long oars.

Before the ship sailed for Constantinople, Juan Gil arrived with the 500 *ducats* for Cervantes' release. The money came from alms at his disposal and from funds designated for Christians he had not been able to find. After having been a captive for five years, Miguel de Cervantes was finally set free.

However, before Cervantes left for Spain, he had some business to complete with the man who had betrayed him, Blanco de Paz.

During the time the friars were negotiating prisoner releases, including Cervantes', Blanco de Paz pretended to be a general commissary of the Inquisition. He prepared a file on Cervantes' activities in Algiers by bribing witnesses to give evidence against him. Blanco de Paz's reason for doing this was to make anything Cervantes might say about him later on seem untrue. Paz wanted to be able to restore his own reputation by assailing Cervantes' character.

Cervantes countered by organizing official documents of exoneration and by accusing Blanco de Paz of treachery. Twelve witnesses testified to the validity of the documents that Cervantes wrote. They depicted Cervantes as a good and honorable man who was popular among the prisoners for his kindness and his unfailing courage in shielding them from punishment. On October 22, 1580, Juan Gil also testified to Cervantes' good character and confirmed the truth of Cervantes' documents.

Once the character inquiry was completed, Cervantes sailed for Spain on October 24, 1580, along with five other ransomed Christians. He had been away from Spain for 10 years. The Captive in *Don Quixote* says, "There is in my opinion no joy on earth comparable to regaining the liberty one has lost." Undoubtedly, Cervantes knew how profoundly accurate these words were.

5

Missions in Andalusia: The Royal Commissions

They saw before them their longed-for, beloved homeland. Joy revived in their hearts; their spirits became excited with new contentment, among the greatest one can have in this life: to return after a long captivity, safe and sound, to one's fatherland.

—Cervantes, *The Generous Suitor*

Cervantes returned to dramatic changes in his Spanish homeland. The population had grown, causing the need for more food, clothing, housing, and other essentials. Rents and prices had skyrocketed. The already large gap between the rich and the poor had increased. Property was concentrated in the hands of the wealthy who could afford to pay the inflated prices. The landowners and the rich merchants prospered. The middle class—small traders, minor officials, and professionals—was hit the hardest. Their incomes did not cover their expenses. The wages of the peasants, who were responsible for the main burden of taxation, did not meet

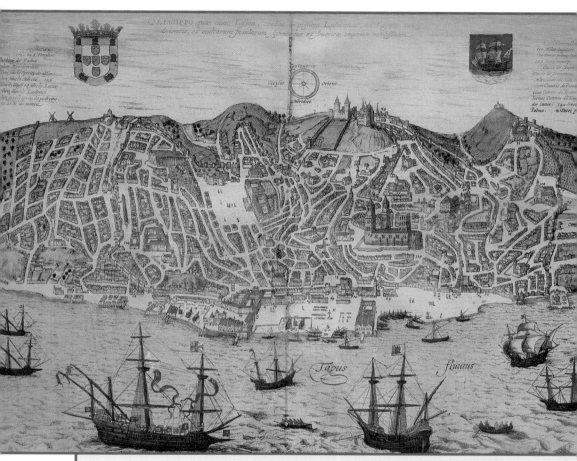

Drastic changes, caused by a population explosion, welcomed Cervantes in his homeland of Spain after five years in prison. While the landowners and rich merchants continued to thrive, the middle class and peasantry suffered because their wages did not increase with the skyrocketing cost of living. The unfortunate circumstances of Cervantes' family members contributed to an already depressing homecoming for Cervantes.

the cost of the increased prices; an increased number of citizens became beggars and prostitutes. This changed economic climate hit Cervantes' father very hard because people could not afford his services as a sergeon.

Cervantes was 33 years old, out of prison, and out of military service. He needed a job to support himself and to pay the debts he had incurred during his years in prison. While in captivity, Cervantes had taken loans to buy food, and he owed money to the Trinitarians for the extra ransom they paid. All he had to show for the previous 10 years was a mutilated left hand and a long list of debts. He spent his first month in Valencia attempting to settle his debts.

After a month, Cervantes traveled to Madrid to reunite with his family. Although he was excited to see his family after so many years away from them, he was saddened by the changes that occurred in their lives while he was imprisoned. His aging father had sold all his possessions to raise funds for his sons' ransoms and could no longer support himself. His mother was stuck with the expensive trading license to sell goods in Algiers that she had hoped would help with his ransom. Miguel's brother, Rodrigo, had re-enlisted in the military and was serving in Portugal. His two sisters, Andrea and Magdalena, were living elsewhere, presumably with lovers. It was a very depressing homecoming.

Cervantes sent a written petition asking for financial help to the Council of Castile. The council denied his request because he was only one of thousands of ex-soldiers seeking a pension. Cervantes was disappointed that, despite his heroic military service, the council would not help his family.

By the time Cervantes decided to present himself in person at court to plead for financial support and work, Philip II, the Spanish king, had moved the seat of the government to Portugal so he could supervise the integration of the newly acquired country into the Spanish empire. The court moved with him.

Out of desperation, Cervantes followed Philip II to Portugal to request a veteran's stipend from the king's representatives. However, the king needed funds for other efforts such as fighting the Dutch and defending against attacks from English pirates in the Atlantic. Also other families were asking for financial help to ransom their sons who were still in prison.

Finally, in May 1581, Cervantes received a temporary appointment as the king's messenger. He crossed the Mediterranean to deliver the king's letters to the governor of Orán, Don Martin de Córdoba. After a successful mission as a courier, he returned to Lisbon, Portugal, at the end of June. Once again, he was unemployed and without money. In November, he requested a post in the New World, which was denied.

By 1582, Cervantes was back in Madrid. His mother and sisters meagerly supported him. In a letter written to Lord Antonio de Eraso on February 17, 1582, Cervantes acknowledged his disappointment that no posts were available for him. In his letter, Cervantes mentioned that he was writing a novel, *La Galatea.* While waiting for news of an appointment, he had returned to his love of writing.

In Madrid, Cervantes became a part of a circle of playwrights, poets, and writers, some of whom he had met in his youth and others in the military. He completed his first novel, *La Galatea,* in 1583. It was a pastoral novel, a popular genre. The pastoral novel presented stories of shepherds and country folks, and included love affairs, killings, and melodramatic events. They were considered escape novels, because they offered distraction from hard times in Spain.

Between 1583 and 1587, Cervantes wrote between 20 and 30 plays. However, he did not make enough money from these writings to support himself.

In November 1584, Cervantes' mother finally received the profits from the 2,000 *ducats* worth of merchandise she had been given permission to export to Algiers. With this money, the debt to the Trinitarians for Cervantes' ransom was paid.

During 1583 and 1584, Cervantes had several important events occur in his life. First, he had an affair with Ana Franca de Rojas, whose husband owned a tavern frequented by actors and playwrights in Madrid. She became pregnant and delivered Cervantes' only confirmed child, Isabel de Saavedra.

On June 14, 1584, he sold his manuscript *La Galatea* to a bookseller named Blas de Robles for 120 *ducats.* He was satisfied with the price, since this was his first novel. At last he had become a bona fide writer.

In September 1584, Miguel went to Esquivias, a village south of Madrid, to help the widow of his friend, the poet Pedro Laínez, edit and publish Laínez's last works. While there, he came to know and love the plains of southern Castile. This area, known as La Mancha, had gently rolling hills, vineyards, wheatfields, and windmills. La Mancha would later become the setting for his most famous novel *The Ingenious Gentleman Don Quixote de la Mancha*.

While in Esquivias, Cervantes met and married Doña Catalina de Salazar. Cervantes was 37 and Catalina was 19. After a two-month courtship, Catalina's uncle, Father Juan de Palacios, married them on December 12, 1584. Their wedding was in the small country church of St. Mary of the Assumption in the town of Esquivias. Miguel's parents were old and could not travel to the wedding. At the time of their marriage, Catalina was still mourning the death of her father, who had died shortly before she met Cervantes. Her mother did not

MIGUEL DE CERVANTES SAAVEDRA

When Cervantes sent his memo to the Council of the Indies on May 21, 1590, he signed his name "Miguel de Cervantes Saavedra." From this point on, he adds this name to his surname. Saavedra came from a distant relation, Gonzalo de Cervantes Saavedra. Gonzalo is listed among the poets mentioned in "Song of Calliope," and so it is assumed that Miguel knew him.

Cervantes gave the name to a heroic captive in the *Romancero*, and to a Christian slave in *Life in Algiers*. He also named his defender of Orán "Saavedra" in *The Gallant Spaniard*. He used the same name in *Don Quixote* for the Christian slave who resisted Hassan Pasha's threats. Miguel de Cervantes Saavedra was the name he used when he wrote *Don Quxiote*.

His daughter, Isabel, born to Ana Franca de Rojas, used this name for several years.

attend the wedding, perhaps because it was too soon after her husband's death.

The marriage of Cervantes to Catalina has been curious to biographers. He brought considerable debt and no certainty of a financial future to the marriage. He was almost twice her age and had traveled extensively. Catalina was from a family of moderate means; they owned some land, but were not wealthy. Her father and mother were unable to sign their names, an indication that they were poorly educated. However, Catalina could read and write. There is evidence that she had a trace of Jewish blood in her ancestry, which was a problem for strict Catholics.

Catalina had three things in her favor—her youth, the small parcels of land she inherited, and the promise of additional land she would inherit after her mother died. However, when Catalina's father died in 1584, he left debts. Cervantes probably did not know about the debts when he married her.

The newlyweds moved into a small two-story house in Esquivias. Part of the marriage procedure in sixteenth century Spain dictated that the husband pay money to his wife's family, and the wife's family provide a dowry of property. In August 1586, even though he was not living with his wife, Cervantes was in Esquivias to receive Catalina's dowry. In return, he paid 100 *ducats* as a marriage settlement. The inventory that was drawn up that day included land, olive trees, vines, hens, a rooster, and a kitchen garden. Cervantes' mother-in-law also gave Cervantes power to administer the family property.

It is thought that Catalina's grieving mother was not excited about her daughter's marriage to a poor, struggling writer, almost 40, with a withered left hand. However, Catalina's mother was a widow who had to raise two young sons of seven and three. Cervantes promise of 100 *ducats* as a marriage settlement was too good to turn down.

When Cervantes arrived in Esquivias, he thought he had

found a peaceful haven—a simple country life, Catalina's fresh young face, rich wine, and noble families. But before long he missed connecting with other writers and business associates. Cervantes started commuting regularly to Madrid and other towns.

A complicating factor in their marriage may have been that shortly before the wedding his previous lover, Ana Franca de Rojas, delivered his illegitimate daughter, Isabel. It is not known if his wife Catalina knew of Cervantes' relationship with Ana and the child that was born from it at that time. Unfortunately, Cervantes and his wife would not be able to have children of their own.

Cervantes' novel, *La Galatea*, was published in 1585 and became popular among his literary friends. What Blas de Robles had paid Cervantes for *La Galatea* was a good price, but since most of it went to pay his debts, it was not enough to live by. By 1587 it was clear to Cervantes that he could not earn a living as a writer.

At this point in history, England and the Protestant movement were growing in strength and influence. The English were posing major problems for Spanish shipping. In April 1587, the English, led by Sir Francis Drake, raided a Spanish port. They destroyed or captured 20 to 30 ships, stealing the cargo the ships carried. This act provoked the Spanish king, Philip II, to attack England. Philip II ordered the mobilization of the Spanish military. The military needed ships, troops, and supplies. The king appointed Antonio de Guevara commissary general, whose job it would be to collect the supplies.

In 1587, Cervantes was in Seville. Diego de Valdivia, Guevara's deputy, was appointing commissary officers to obtain supplies for the gathering fleet. He appointed Cervantes to the post of commissioner of supplies for the Spanish Armada, and assigned him to the Andalusian region. In this post, Cervantes was to obtain corn, wheat, oil, and other needed supplies for the war effort. After he acquired

In response to the English raid of a Spanish port, King Philip II ordered his Spanish naval fleet to mobilize. Cervantes was appointed to a commissary post to secure supplies as part of the fleet's preparations. After acquiring supplies including corn, wheat, and oil, Cervantes organized their storage, measurement, and shipment. He was also responsible for securing payment to the farmers for their crops.

these supplies, he had to arrange for their storage, measurement and shipment, and request payment for the crops. However, Cervantes was not the one responsible for actually paying the farmers. As commissary, Cervantes had extensive power and responsibility, including judicial power when necessary to confiscate goods and to arrest those resisting the acquisition of the supplies. When Cervantes took this job he didn't realize he was starting a life of wandering that would last nearly 15 years.

His first assignment was to obtain wheat at a village called Écija. Serious problems developed. The crop was poor, the government had not made payments for previous shipments, and local authorities wanted to keep their crops for local consumption. Consequently, Cervantes faced considerable hostility in fulfilling his responsibilities. His personality lacked the necessary toughness the job demanded. He faced an impossible situation. The local town council had passed legislation calling for the town to provide less of their crops than the amount the government requested. After unsuccessful negotiations with Cervantes to reduce the amounts requested, the town leaders went over his head to his boss, Valdivia, seeking relief. Valdivia refused their request and ordered Cervantes to collect the crops.

Cervantes set about the task of gathering the supplies. He decided to take larger amounts from those who had the biggest quantity. This included supplies belonging to the Catholic Church in Seville. The vicar general of Seville excommunicated Cervantes for his actions. Cervantes, who considered himself a good Catholic, was deeply troubled. However, excommunications were common in those days, as church leaders continually ran into conflicts with civil authorities.

After Cervantes' excommunication, his boss, Valdivia, came to Écija and worked out a compromise with the townspeople for the supplies, and the government returned some of their crops.

Cervantes traveled to another town, Castro del Rio, to obtain goods. When a resistant church official refused to turn over the requested supplies, Cervantes imprisoned him. He was excommunicated again, this time by the vicar of Córdoba for imprisoning a church official.

Life as a commissary was hard for Cervantes, filled with a variety of unpleasant duties—from seizing crops and handing out prison sentences to explaining why the government was slow to play for the confiscated goods.

When Cervantes returned to Madrid, he faced another

disappointment: he was not paid for his services. The 1,300 *maravedis* owed to him had not been deposited in his account by the government. The good news, to his relief, was that his mother was living comfortably, safe from need. Ana Franca de Rojas, his former mistress and mother of his child, was now a widow and kept her husband's tavern on Francos Street while she raised her two daughters.

In January, Antonio de Guevara renewed Cervantes' commission. Between January to May 1588, Cervantes was traveling again between Écija and the surrounding towns. This time he was gathering olive oil. He had gained valuable experience and insight in his previous work with farmers and reduced the amount of supplies required by half. The farmers were very pleased and put him in charge of collecting taxes demanded for the treasury. This was a strong statement of their confidence in Cervantes. However, the position itself was full of potential trouble—nobody likes a tax collector.

Cervantes lived a very basic existence because the government had not paid him all he had earned. Although struggling financially, Cervantes did not resort to tactics used by some commissaries who illegally supported themselves by selling government supplies for personal profit. Though Cervantes was honest, his poor bookkeeping records would later haunt his government work.

With debts mounting, Cervantes had to take to the road again. He traveled back to Écija. This time he was not only to store the requisitioned wheat, he was also supposed to have it ground and made into biscuits. In the heat of the summer, Cervantes discovered that the crops from the previous season were filled with weevils because they had not been stored properly and could not be used for food. The farmers, who had reluctantly given up their crops, were outraged that their precious goods were so poorly managed.

Meanwhile, word came to Spain that their fleet was defeating the English and landing on English shores. The Spanish

Cervantes visited farmers of olive groves in Écija and surrounding towns to gather olive oil in 1588. Responding to the limited capabilities of the poor farmers, Cervantes reduced the number of olives that the farmers were required to supply to the state by half. The farmers reciprocated by selecting Cervantes as their tax collector, an enormous show of their confidence in him.

people were elated. But the news was false. Eventually, the citizens learned that the defeated Spanish Armada had retreated to Spain. Only half the ships and troops returned safely.

King Philip II was convinced that the Spanish fleet had been defeated by delays in departures, weather problems, leadership inadequacies, and ill-prepared troops. He decided the

Spanish fleet should attack the English again the next year and ordered the military to prepare.

New war preparations kept the commissaries working. Between January and April 1589, Miguel continued his commissary work, spending most of his time between Écija and Seville.

Cervantes was tired of arranging the purchase of supplies for the military. Negotiating purchases, making compromises, and taking judicial action when necessary became a great burden. In addition, he still was not rewarded with regular pay, which caused continued financial difficulties. He decided to change his plight by applying for a position in the Indies, the Spanish possessions in the New World—America. On May 21, 1590, he sent a petition to the Council of Indies, stating:

> Sir: Miguel de Cerbantes Sahavedra [*sic*] . . . requests and begs with all humility that Your Majesty will deign to reward him with one of the three or four posts that are at present vacant in the Indies: viz., the auditor's office in the kingdom of New Granada, or the governorship of the province of Soconusco in Guatemala, or the post of accountant of galleys at Cartagena (in modern Colombia), or magistrate of the city of La Paz (in modern Bolivia) . . .

He said he would serve in any of the open positions and mentioned that he was a "capable and competent man, deserving of Your Majesty's favor." He added that he wanted to end his days serving the king as his ancestors had done.

Although Cervantes served his country, first in war as a military soldier, then as a government servant, he had four things against him. He had been rejected before when he petitioned for similar work in the Americas; he was older than most men who were assigned to such positions; his withered left hand was considered a handicap; and his recent government service was under a leader whose financial practices were being investigated for corruption.

On June 6, 1590, the secretary of the council rejected his request for an assignment in America and jotted on the margin of his request, "Let him look around Castile for some kind of government post." This was a big disappointment to Cervantes, who blamed the rejection on government corruption. He believed those with influence and money received the posts.

Discouraged by his rejection, Cervantes requested full pay for his government service. He was offered half of what the government owed him and he refused to accept lesser payment. He appealed the offer, and on March 12, 1592, he was paid most of his back pay.

During this time, his former commissary general, Guevara, was under investigation for fraud. The investigation led to the arrest of Guevara and some of his subordinates. The judicial investigation cleared Guevara, but some of his subordinates were found guilty and were hanged in December 1592. Since Cervantes worked for these individuals, there were some suspicions about his own financial activities. He was summoned to Madrid to account for how he had handled requisitions. Since he couldn't afford to travel, he sent a representative who was able to clear his name.

A new commissary general, Pedro de Isunza, was appointed to the post in Seville. Cervantes continued working for him. The new commissary general reduced Cervantes' salary. In May 1591, Cervantes left for Jaen to purchase olive oil and wheat. He traveled through other towns in the region, obtaining wheat and barley.

One of Cervantes' assistants clashed with a steward in charge of the royal granaries in Teba over irregularities connected with a grain seizure. The steward felt Cervantes' assistant had treated him unfairly and appealed to the king to request payment for damages. Cervantes was held responsible for his assistant's actions. However, his general, Isunza, wrote a letter to the king, defending Cervantes' honesty, and the king suspended the charges.

There were other incidents in his next assignments that led to further charges filed against Cervantes. One town claimed that he was illegally selling wheat, and another said his accounts were irregular. He was imprisoned for the first charge until Isunza intervened on his behalf.

The Council of War in Madrid began to question Cervantes' honesty and service. Cervantes' previous work for a corrupt commissary general, his own work record, plus his assistant's problems in Teba made Cervantes a character of suspicion. The council summoned Cervantes to appear before them, but after hearing his testimony, they let him go.

During his government service, Cervantes spent about half his time in Seville where he recovered from his travels, prepared his defense against charges, and requested payment of his salary. Seville was the capital of the Andalusia region and the center of power for the area. Known as the "marketplace of the world," Seville received shipments of merchandise from foreign ports. Spain was becoming dependent on foreign imports.

In the spring of 1594, King Philip II decided to terminate the commissary system. Cervantes had been working as a commissary for about seven years. By the time his commissions ended, he had traveled through at least six Andalusian provinces and crisscrossed the Sierra Morena Mountains and the plains of La Mancha to Toledo, Esquivias, and Madrid. Bad roads, weather, and lodgings, poor food, and irritable people had been part of his adventures. The many nights in country inns taught him about life in a way that a university never could.

Out of work, Cervantes returned to Madrid in June 1594. He found a new job as tax collector in August. Cervantes must have known this wouldn't be an easy job as people hate to give up their money.

His task was to collect a very large sum of money (2.5 million *maravedis*) in back taxes owed by citizens in the Granada region. He had to visit about 10 cities and negotiate with the officials for the money.

Because Cervantes' own personal credit wasn't good, he was required to provide a surety bond (guarantee) of 1,500,000 *maravedis*. He received financial backing from someone who trusted his reputation. In addition, he and his wife had to commit their possessions as a show of good faith. His wages would come from the taxes he collected and were set at 550 *maravedis* per day, which was twice as much as he had earned in his last job.

Though Cervantes often made his collections without a problem, in some towns, the officials stalled. Still others claimed that they had already paid some of the taxes to the treasury and produced receipts showing the payments. Complaints caused delays. Each time he collected the tax money, he sent it to Madrid.

Finally, he managed to collect the full amount due in every town except three. In Velez Malaga, he collected 130,000 *maravedis* out of the 277,000 they owed. For safekeeping, he decided to deposit the tax money collected plus some money of his own in a Seville bank owned by the merchant Simon Freire. Freire gave him a money order he could cash in Madrid.

When Cervantes reached Madrid, he waited for Freire to forward the money. There he learned that this bank had gone bankrupt, Freire had disappeared with 60,000 *ducats*, and all funds were frozen. Cervantes' world was crashing down around him.

After considerable effort, Cervantes was able to recover the money from Freire's estate. It was deposited in the treasury in January 1597. The king ordered Cervantes to pay all the expenses that resulted from the bankruptcy. Cervantes never received his personal money; the treasurer kept it.

Once the account with Freire was settled, Cervantes should have returned to Madrid to present a detailed balance sheet of his work, but he did not do that. His time as a tax collector was a financial disaster and his work for the government ended. Again, Cervantes was out of work.

In the summer of 1597, the general accountant's office demanded Cervantes pay 80,000 *maravedis* to cover the missing tax from Velez Malaga. Since there was no report from Cervantes telling about the tax reduction, the treasury wanted the money they assumed he had collected. The king ordered Cervantes to appear at court within 20 days to explain his accounts and told Cervantes to post bond at his own expense.

A judge in Seville notified Cervantes that his guarantors must cover his debt. If Cervantes could not come up with the money, he was to be taken to Madrid and put under lock and key. However, instead of charging Cervantes for the 80,000 *maravedis*, the judge demanded two and a half (2.5) million *maravedis*, the entire amount of tax Cervantes was commissioned to collect. The judge expected him to pay an amount far beyond what was due. Cervantes had already returned most of the collected money to the treasury. With no way for Cervantes to raise such a large sum, the judge had him arrested and jailed in Seville, ignoring the king's order to send Cervantes to Madrid to be jailed.

At age 50, Cervantes' seven-month imprisonment came 20 years after the Turks took him prisoner in Algiers. Cervantes felt anger and indignation at his treatment. When he was in prison in Algiers, the enemies of his country and his religion had imprisoned him. This time, his own people held him captive.

Although Seville was a major center for commerce, it had also become home to an underworld consisting of organizations that specialized in delinquency and crime. Members in these brotherhoods were frustrated farmers, unemployed clothing manufacturers, and disillusioned citizens from noble birth, commoners and professional killers. The Seville prison was filled beyond capacity. In prison, Cervantes experienced a different side of life in Seville. One eyewitness described the prison as "a true picture of hell on earth," because of the terrible conditions—stench, chaos, confusion, and violence.

Veteran prisoners initiated newcomers with brutal

King Philip II responded to Cervantes' letter, which outlined the injustices of the trial and sentence for his alleged mishandling of tax revenue, by ordering for Cervantes' release in 1597. For reasons unknown, the judge did not uphold the king's order, and Cervantes was not released from prison until the following year. Cervantes never returned to the courts to settle his accounts.

practices to test their courage. Prisoners with money could purchase fine clothing, food, lovers, and other privileges not available to those without funds. Prisoners shouted cheers for others who were being tortured for refusing to name accomplices. Mourning and funerals took place regularly for those condemned to death.

Without funds, Cervantes would have no privileges and limited rations of food. He was not able to pay ransom for his release and had little hope for justice.

Cervantes wrote a letter to King Philip II outlining the unfair trial and sentence. On December 1, 1597, King Philip II ordered Cervantes to be released from prison and told him to appear in Madrid in 30 days to give an account of how he had handled funds. However, the king's letter said that even if he did not meet the conditions, he was still to be freed. For some reason the judge did not release Cervantes.

Finally, at the end of March 1598, while Cervantes was still in prison, royal accountants sent a new summons from the treasury. They asked Cervantes for a sworn statement regarding the wheat and barley collected in 1591, when he had been a commissary. Cervantes told them he could do that only if they would release him from jail so he could consult his records. They finally released Cervantes from prison in April 1598. On April 28, 1598, he submitted a sworn statement telling how he handled his commission in 1591. He never went to Madrid to fulfill the conditions spelled out in the king's letter. After his release, treasury agents twice attempted to have him tried and imprisoned, but their efforts were futile.

6

To Dream the Impossible Dream: The Writer

And the world will be better for this
that one man, scorned and covered with scars,
still strove with his last ounce of courage
to reach the unreachable stars!

—Joe Darion, "Man of La Mancha"

From the time of Miguel de Cervantes' first sonnet in 1566 at the birth of Princess Catalina Micaela until his death in 1616, he wrote. He didn't belong to fashionable literary circles. He was always short of money and looking for employment that would put food on the table. His writings weren't popular. The court never gave him the official recognition and approval customary for literary greats at the time. However, his days as a chamberlain and soldier, his imprisonments, the minor government jobs, and his debt provided a rich and exciting tapestry that he used as a backdrop for his writing. Undoubtedly, Cervantes would have been surprised to learn that he

This portrait of Cervantes, painted many years after his death, depicts him as a gifted writer—quill pen in hand and surrounded by books. In no way does it depict how Cervantes spent most of his adult years—impoverished, looking for work, or in prison.

is now considered both a remarkable Spanish writer and one of the world's great literary geniuses.

In order to talk about Miguel de Cervantes the writer, we

need to go back to 1582, the point in his life where he seriously turned to writing not only to express his artistic abilities, but also to earn a living.

Cervantes' work on the novel *La Galatea* began while he was staying with his family in Madrid in 1582. He went to Madrid hoping for a post from the government. While Cervantes waited for an appointment, he went to his old hangouts to renew friendships with his literary acquaintances— Francisco de Figueroa, Pedro Laínez, Juan Ruft—and made new friends in the literary community. In the meantime, he started working on *La Galatea,* a story of love and marriage, in which he mentions many of these poets.

Cervantes felt timid as he began writing *La Galatea*. As a storyteller, Cervantes wanted to surprise or astonish readers by unexpected changes in his story or unexpected actions by his characters. He experimented with mixing what the characters "believed" to be true with what actually was.

In 1584, Cervantes found a publisher for *La Galatea*, Blas de Robles, who paid him 1,336 *reales* (approximately 121 *ducats*) for the manuscript and the right to publish it. It would be 20 long years before the publication of his next book, *The Ingenious Gentleman Don Quixote de la Mancha.*

After selling *La Galatea*, Cervantes traveled to Esquivias to meet with Juana Gaitan, the widow of his friend Pedro Laínez. Cervantes hoped his name as sponsor would help to get Gaitan's works published. Although Cervantes was married to Catalina de Palacios, he traveled back and forth between Esquivias and Madrid to continue his writing and business contacts.

In 1585, the theater had become a commercial business in Spanish cities, especially Madrid, where two permanent theaters were located. Public support of the theater caused the rapid turnover of productions, providing many opportunities for playwrights. People flocked to the theaters to see the two-and-a-half hour productions. Each production had several parts. First, there was a *loa*, which might be a monologue to prepare the audience for the play, or a short dramatic sketch to get the attention of the audience. As with concerts, where a musical group starts the show, the *loa* was the warm up for the main attraction. Next came the first act of the drama, followed by a comic interlude. Theatergoers at the time knew Cervantes for his interludes. Between the second and third act, there was usually another performance, such as a dance.

On March 5, 1585, Cervantes signed a contract with a theatrical company manager, Gaspar de Porras, for two plays: *The Comedy of Confusion* and *The Treaty of Constantinople and Death of Selim*. It is not likely that Porras would have commissioned these plays if he had not been familiar with Cervantes' previous work. This could mean that Cervantes had already written *The Siege of Numancia* and *The Traffic of Algiers.*

Cervantes was to receive 40 *ducats* for each play, 20 *ducats* up front and 20 *ducats* upon completion. He wrote the first play, *The Comedy of Confusion,* but historians do not know if he ever completed the second.

Between 1583 and 1587, Cervantes wrote between 20 and 30 plays. It looked like his artistic and economic career would be in the theater. Then his career as a playwright suddenly ended. The reason was the emergence of Lope de Vega.

In 1584 Cervantes and Lope de Vega were both in Madrid. They both wrote for the theater and both had connections with a theater company directed by Jeronimo Velázquez. Lope, 15 years younger than Cervantes, was beginning his career. The public already knew Cervantes' writings. Both writers were in love with beautiful women—Cervantes with Ana Franca de Rojas, Vega with Helena de Ossorio.

When Vega published a song in 1584, Cervantes, in a spirit of friendship, wrote a warm eulogy in *La Galatea* to his young colleague. In a play, *The Valencian Widow,* Lope de Vega returned the compliment to Cervantes:

> This then is *La Galatea,*
> Which, if you desire a good book,
> You have but to ask for it.
> Its author was Miguel Cervantes,
> Who in Lepanto lost
> A hand. . .

However, it was here that the paths of the two men began to separate. Cervantes began his career for the government, which left Lope de Vega, his junior, with no other competition.

By 1609, they were archrivals. In a stinging sonnet aimed at Cervantes, Lope de Vega wrote:

> Spare me other verses like those you've put together by pilfering from Ariosto and Garcilaso . . . and for pity's sake don't begin to write in four languages: inasmuch as you jot down inanities only, there's danger that a sea of stupidities may make the rounds in as many as four nations!

Their animosity may have had creative reasons. Their ideas about the rules governing writing for the theater were total opposites. In Part I, Chapter 48 of *Don Quixote,* the canon of Toledo says that the popular plays were "notorious nonsense, monsters without feet or head."

Vega started writing for the Madrid theaters in the 1580s. His action-packed dramas with a nationalist flavor deserted the old, traditional way of writing. The people loved him. Lope de Vega, and those who chose to write like him, became the most popular playwrights.

Cervantes could not bring himself to approve the works of Lope de Vega, who Cervantes felt was willing to sell his plays, even if the writing was inferior, just to earn money. The public, however, did not think Lope de Vega's plays were inferior. He was their idol. With his popularity, he became conceited and arrogant. In a poem he compared himself to Homer and Virgil, who were considered to be the greatest writers at the time, and said he was their equal. Luis de Góngora, a great poet, wrote on the document that is preserved in the National Library of Madrid: "If you say this of yourself, my dear Lopino (Lope), you are an artless, brainless idiot."

Cervantes tried to persuade commercial theater operators to return to the pre-De Vega drama, *his* drama. Unfortunately, the managers of plays were no longer interested in buying. Before long, the plays of Lope de Vega were the only ones produced at the theaters.

By 1587 Cervantes needed to earn a decent living. He went to Seville where his 15 years of wandering as a businessman began.

Cervantes' literary works from these years are limited to a few poems. In the summer of 1588, news of the defeat of the Spanish Armada filtered into Spain. Cervantes found it hard to accept the rumors and wrote his first ode to the Armada expressing confidence in the brave sword of Catholicism. His images showed his faith in the Catholic troops who would overcome the dissenters. However, when the defeat of the Armada was confirmed, he wrote a second ode, consoling and compassionate, full of optimism that when the Spaniards gathered their strength, they would again be victorious.

In between the commissary jobs he held between 1590 and 1593, Cervantes may have begun to work on some of the great texts he would publish later. *A Captive's Tale*, based on memories of Algiers, may have been written around 1590. It later became part of *Don Quixote*. During this time, he also composed miscellaneous poems.

On September 5, 1592, he signed a contract to write six plays for Rodrigo Osorio in return for 300 *ducats*. Osorio was a prominent actor and the director of a troupe, but it appears that Cervantes did not write the plays. In 1593 his ballad, "The House of Jealousy," was published anonymously.

Somewhere between 1592 and 1598, Cervantes may have written an early version of *Rinconete and Cortadillo*. Cervantes wondered what would happen if he used dialogue and comic realism in this novel. It would be an experiment. The story would deal with the Sevillian lowlife Cervantes knew rather well. In the story, two boys go to Seville and join a gang of thieves; by the story's end, they criticize their adventures with the gang, but they remain with the gang for several months. The book was eventually part of a collection of books published around 1613.

In the spring of 1595, the Dominicans of Zaragoza organized a poetry contest. Cervantes won and received three silver spoons as his prize. He was delighted, yet he chose not to accept the awards in person. He sent someone to pick up his prize, and instead he went to Toledo for the ordination of one of his brothers-in-law.

In 1597, Cervantes was arrested and thrown in the prison of Seville for being unable to account for the lost tax money he collected. His *Exemplary Novels* provided the most colorful picture of the underworld that existed in Seville, people he must have met in prison. He painted the picaresque world as a life of freedom, uninhibited by the rules of church and state.

During the forced inactivity of prison life, he felt the desire to write. This may have been the time when he developed the basic idea for *Don Quixote*.

Once out of prison, Cervantes may have left Seville in 1600 and headed toward Toledo and Esquivias. He may have been living a more settled life, writing and traveling between Madrid, Toledo, and Esquivias, finally spending time with his wife.

Only two documented occasions provide a clue to his whereabouts from 1600 to 1604. On August 19, 1600, in Toledo, Cervantes' brother-in-law Fernando de Salazar

Palacios, who had decided to become a Franciscan monk, wrote a will leaving his possessions to his sister, Catalina, and his elder brother. He designated Cervantes as executor. So, Cervantes was most likely present at the ordination. The other occasion was a baptism in January 1602 in Esquivias, where Cervantes became a godfather.

One can assume that between 1600 and 1604, Cervantes was working on his novel *Don Quixote*. Wherever he lived during this time, he was inventing the great adventure of Don Quixote and his squire, Sancho Panza, on their journey south toward the Sierra Morena.

In 1604, he found a publisher for *Don Quixote*. Cervantes was delighted when Francisco de Robles, the son and successor of Blas de Robles, who years before had published *La Galatea*, agreed to buy his manuscript.

In August, Cervantes gave his manuscript to Robles, who paid him about 1,500 *reales*. Juan de la Cuesta printed the book in Madrid. By December, the last pages were coming off the presses.

Cervantes moved to Valladolid to give his new book publicity. A few weeks later, Catalina left Esquivias and joined him. They would stay together until Cervantes' death.

Seven years had passed since Cervantes first developed the idea for *Don Quixote*—years filled with disruptions— prison, moving from place to place, fights with creditors, and family problems. When asked why he wrote it, Cervantes replied, "to cause mankind to abhor the false and foolish tales of the books of chivalry."

Before the book reached the bookstores, Lope de Vega wrote a nasty letter to a friend saying, "there is not one as bad as Cervantes, nor so stupid as to praise *Don Quixote*."

When at last *Don Quixote* reached the bookstores in March 1605, the public loved it. Robles and Cuesta began immediately to work on a second edition. Cervantes gave Robles exclusive permission to print and sell the book. Pirated editions began to appear. By April, Robles was preparing to

EL INGENIOSO
HIDALGO DON QVI-
XOTE DE LA MANCHA,

Compuesto por Miguel de Ceruantes
Saauedra.

DIRIGIDO AL DVQVE DE BEIAR,
Marques de Gibraleon, Conde de Benalcaçar, y Baña-
res, Vizconde de la Puebla de Alcozer, Señor de
las villas de Capilla, Curiel, y
Burguilios.

Año,   1605.

CON PRIVILEGIO,
EN MADRID, Por Iuan de la Cuesta.

Véndese en casa de Francisco de Robles, librero del Rey nto señor.

Titel der ersten Auflage des „Don Quijote" von Miguel de
Cervantes Saavedra, Madrid 1605

Title Page of the First Edition of „Don Quixote", Madrid 1605

The first edition of Cervantes' *Don Quixote* was published in Madrid
in 1605. Francisco de Robles, son of the same man who had
published Cervantes' *La Galatea*, purchased the manuscript. The
book became an immediate bestseller, even finding success in
the Spanish colonies in America. Perhaps the greatest testaments
to the book's popularity were the pirated copies and bogus sequels
that followed *Don Quixote's* printing.

take legal actions against his dishonest colleagues who were printing and selling *Don Quixote*. By June, Robles was shipping *Don Quixote* to the Spanish colonies in America. In just three months, it had broken all sales records. At last, Cervantes felt the excitement and satisfaction that came with fame. Later, through Part II of *Don Quixote*, Cervantes expresses his delight at the book's appeal to all kinds of people:

> Children finger it; young people read it; grown men know it by heart, and old men praise it. It is so dog-eared, in fact, and so familiar to all sorts of people that whenever they see a lean horse go by, they cry: "There goes Rocinante (Quixote's horse)."

During his two years in Valladolid, Cervantes' success as a writer inspired him to write more. He began writing and collecting stories which were published later under the title of *Exemplary Novels*. He based another story, *The Colloquy of the Dogs,* on the imaginary conversation of two watchdogs at a hospital in Valladolid. One dog tells of his journey from master to master. In his travels, he found the world was full of wickedness and deceit.

During the last 10 years of Cervantes' life, he completed five books: four published in his lifetime and one after his death. During these years, Cervantes had several projects going at the same time—poetry, drama, and several prose works. Part II of *Don Quixote* was just one of his tasks.

In the prologue to his *Exemplary Novels,* published in 1613, he wrote:

> I have given these stories the title of Exemplary; and if you look closely there is not one of them that does not afford a useful example. . . . If I believed that the reading of these *Novels* would in any way arouse an evil thought or desire, I would sooner cut off the hand that wrote them than see them published.

The Journey to Parnassus was a poem in eight chapters that told the journey by land and by sea to Mount Parnassus, where a great battle took place between the good poets and the bad. It was published in 1614.

At last, Cervantes plunged into finishing the second part of *Don Quixote.* He had reached Chapter 36 of Part II by July 1614.

In October 1614, a bogus second part of *Don Quixote* appeared. It was titled *Second Tome of the Ingenious Gentleman Don Quixote de la Mancha, Which Contains His Third Departure: and It Is the Fifth Part of His Adventures.* When Cervantes heard of the pirated version, he had already finished Chapter 58.

The author of the counterfeit book was Alonso Fernandez de Avellaneda. In those days, there were no copyright laws, so an author had no legal way to prosecute someone who stole his works. Cervantes would have ignored the pirated version, but Avellaneda wrote a scathing preface to the book personally attacking Cervantes. He mocked Cervantes for being old, for having lost the use of his left hand, for his prison years, for being poor and friendless, and for being jealous of Lope de Vegas' success.

When Cervantes investigated, he discovered Alonso Fernandez de Avellaneda was a pseudonym used by an unknown author. He also discovered that the publisher listed was old and ill and had long before stopped his publishing business.

Spurred by fury and indignation at the appearance of the false *Don Quixote,* Cervantes rushed to finish his own book. By February 1615 he had written 38 more chapters in seven months. However, the effort exhausted him, and his health began to fail.

To assure that no one else would write a novel about Don Quixote, Cervantes killed him off. In the final paragraph of Part II he said:

> For me alone Don Quixote was born and I for him. His was the power of action, mine of writing. Only we two are at one, despite that fictitious and Tordillescan scribe (Avellaneda) who has dared, and may dare again, to pen the deeds of my valorous knight . . . and should you chance to make his

(Avellaneda's) acquaintance, you may tell him to leave Don Quixote's weary and mouldering bones to rest in the grave . . . where he most certainly lies, stretched at full length and powerless to make a third journey . . .

Part II of *The Ingenious Gentleman Don Quixote de la Mancha* was on sale by the middle of November 1615.

WORKS OF MIGUEL DE CERVANTES

	PUBLISHED
Early Plays	
Life in Algiers (printed 1784)	
Numantia (printed 1784)	
Battle of Lepanto	1584
The Perplexed Lady	1587
The High-spirited Arsinda	
La Galatea	1585
Don Quixote	
Part I	1605
Part II	1615
Exemplary Novels	1613
The Little Gypsy	
The Generous Lover	
Rinconete and Cortadillo	
The Anglo-Spanish Lady	
The Glass Licentiate	
The Power of Blood	
The Jealous Estremaduran	
The Illustrious Kitchen-maid	
The Two Maidens	
Lady Cornelia	
The Fraudulent Marriage	
Dialogue Between Scipio and Berganza	
(also called *The Colloquy of the Dogs*)	
The Pretended Aunt	

WORKS OF MIGUEL DE CERVANTES (continued)

Journey to Parnassus	1614
Addendum to the Parnassus	
Eight Plays and Eight New Interludes	1615
Plays:	
The Prisons of Algiers	
The Great Sultana	
The Gallant Spaniard	
The Labyrinth of Love	
The House of Jealousy and Forest of Arden	
The Fortunate Procurer	
Pedro de Urdemalas	
The Link	
Interludes:	
The Election of the Magistrates of Daganzo	
The Widowed Procurer	
The Divorce Judge	
The Miraculous Reredo	
The Cave of Salamanca	
The Counterfeit Biscayan	
The Vigilant Guardian	
The Jealous Old Man	
The Labors of Persiles and Sigismunda	1617
Unpublished and probably uncompleted works:	
More Than Meets the Eye	
The Weeks in the Garden	
Bernardo	
La Galatea, Part II	

Cervantes started *Don Quixote* as a parody of the chivalric romances that were popular with the Spanish readers. He said his goal in writing this novel was to show that "Don Quixote is a madman whose idealism is folly because it so far exceeds the limits of the possible."

Cervantes' work changed the course of literature. Through

his long story about a mad knight, he made realism and characterization the cornerstones of a novel. He succeeded in creating fully developed characters by using dialogue to show and reveal in subtle ways the inner natures of his characters. His characters actually talked using the speech of real people and listened to each other. Literary critics have given him the title of "Father of the Modern Novel." *Don Quixote* has had wider distribution than any book written except the Bible.

Cervantes hurried to finish his last work, *Labors of Persiles and Sigismunda*. In this fairy tale about two young people in love, Persiles is heir to the kingdom of Thule, and Sigismunda is the daughter of the king of Friesland. The two lovers run away together pretending to be brother and sister. After numerous adventures and travels that take them to many countries, they arrive in Rome and marry.

By March 1616, he had finished the story, except the dedication and prologue. On Tuesday, April 19, he gathered his strength and wrote his last dedication. His prologue was finished by Wednesday. On Friday, April 22, 1616, he died.

7

When the Troubled Spirit May Rest: Death

As to what may be said about all this, my reputation will take care of itself: my friends will take pleasure in repeating such things, which give me an even greater pleasure as I listen to them.
—Cervantes, *Labors of Persiles and Sigismunda*

In the last years of his life, Miguel de Cervantes hoped to find peace at last, the peace that eluded him most of his life. However, his fortune would continue to vary.

Cervantes journeyed to Valladolid in July 1604 to look for a place to rent. He found a three-story house on a street now called the Rastro de Valladolid and rented a second-floor apartment. In front of the house was a little bridge over the Esqueva River. He then returned to Esquivias to help his wife Catalina settle her mother's estate. When Cervantes returned to Valladolid, Catalina went with him.

By late summer, Cervantes' family was settled in their new apartment. He was happy to have his family together, including his wife

In an effort to escape a tarnished reputation for the questionable circumstances surrounding the Ezpeleta affair, Miguel de Cervantes and his family moved from Valladolid to Madrid in 1606. Cervantes would spend the last 10 years of his life in Madrid, writing and rebuilding his relationship with the Catholic Church, which had been severely damaged during his years as a commissary.

Catalina, his sisters Andrea and Magdalena, his niece Constanza, and his daughter Isabel. Andrea and Magdalena earned their living by doing needlework for the wealthy upper class. Like many of their clients, they followed the king's court to its new capital, Valladolid. Twenty people lived in the apartment house, including a gossipy woman named Isabel de Ayala.

The move would be good for Cervantes because his editor, the owner of a bookstore, was in Valladolid, and Cervantes wanted to be around to help with the publicity for his book, *Don Quixote,* which came out in March 1605. He was enjoying his newly found success as the author of *Don Quixote* when bad luck struck again.

On the night of June 27, 1605, two men fought a duel on the little bridge in front of Cervantes' house. A seriously wounded man landed on the front porch of the apartment building where Cervantes lived. Cervantes assisted neighbors in carrying the man into a neighbor's apartment. They contacted a surgeon to sew up his wounds, a sword injury to his right thigh and a deep cut in his lower stomach. A priest heard his confession. Magdalena provided care for the man.

The wounded man was Gaspar de Ezpeleta, a knight in the Order of St. James. He was known in town to be an arrogant playboy. Recently he had participated in a public bullfight, where he made a fool of himself by falling off his horse.

The surgeon informed the local magistrate that the wounds were serious and Ezpeleta might die. The magistrate immediately opened an inquiry to determine what had happened and what charges he should file. The magistrate interviewed Ezpeleta to obtain his story. Ezpeleta said that he had been with a friend earlier in the evening. Around 10:30 P.M., he had decided to stroll through the town. He said that someone had approached him and a fight had occurred. He claimed the fight was fair and would not identify the attacker.

Through questioning, the magistrate learned from Ezpeleta's servants that Ezpeleta was having an affair with a married woman, the wife of Melchor Galvan, a government official. The servants testified that a veiled woman, who was later identified as Melchor Galvan's wife, recently visited at the victim's apartment, seeking two diamond and emerald rings she was missing. The woman's husband was threatening to kill her for losing the rings. When Ezpeleta died a few days later, the rings were found in his pocket along with a folded note that the magistrate kept and never mentioned. Eventually the magistrate returned the rings to the woman.

The magistrate needed to find someone to blame. None of the testimony implicated Cervantes and his family. However, on June 30, the magistrate arrested Cervantes, Andrea, Isabel, and Constanza along with six others. He suspected that one of the women knew more about the incident than she admitted. Adding to his suspicions was the fact that the dying man left a silk nightgown for Magdalena in gratitude for the care she gave him. Then there was the gossipy woman on the third floor, Isabel de Ayala, who complained about men visiting the Cervantes' house at strange hours. Neighbors suspected that Cervantes' daughter, Isabel Saavedra, was entertaining men. The magistrate called in three other magistrates to participate in interviews with the Cervantes family.

After being in prison for a day and a half, the magistrate released Cervantes and the women from prison, but kept them under house arrest. They appealed their case, and the order was dropped 10 days later. This was Cervantes' fourth jail incident. It was the jail in which his father and grandfather had served time years earlier because of their bad debts. Despite the testimony of Ezpeleta's landlady, which implicated Melchor Galvan in the assault, Galvan was never interviewed. A week after the Cervantes family was released, the case was closed.

The Ezpeleta affair tarnished Cervantes' reputation and public image as a great author. He had no reason to stay in Valladolid. In 1606, at age 59, Cervantes and his wife Catalina moved to Madrid. Madrid would be Cervantes' final home.

During his last 10 years, he focused on writing. However, within a short time, another problem confronted Cervantes. His daughter Isabel left home when she married Diego Sanz del Aguila in December 1606. A year later she gave birth to a daughter named Isabel. Two years after their wedding, her husband died.

Juan de Urbina comforted Isabel in her grief. He was a 50-year-old man with good business sense, property, stocks, and real estate. Although he had a wife and family, he was living alone in Madrid. He took a special interest in Isabel. Urbina set her

The statue of Don Quixote in Madrid honors the great author who chose the city as his final home. Though his remaining years in Madrid were not without misfortune, Cervantes was able to make amends with his church and look after his family.

up in a house very close to his house, rented in the name of one of his servants. Some scholars believe that he was having an affair with Isabel.

Isabel did not remain a widow very long. Three months after her first husband's death, she married Luis de Molina. There was strange bargaining about the dowry Isabel would bring into the marriage. Neither Isabel nor her father, Cervantes, had many possessions or any money. Juan de Urbina agreed to provide money for her dowry. Cervantes signed the contract, giving the appearance that he was providing the funds. The house Urbina owned became the property of Isabel's child. However, there was a clause in the contract that Isabel was not aware of: if her child died, the house would become Urbina's property again. Of course no one thought that her child would die.

Unfortunately, and to everyone's surprise, Cervantes' grand-daughter, Isabel, died around March 1610. At the child's death, Urbina wanted to stop paying the money he promised Isabel for the dowry and to reclaim ownership of the house. Isabel and her husband were very upset about these developments, especially when they realized that Cervantes had participated in the agreement. Isabel and her husband took Urbina to court and spent many years fighting legal battles until all of his commitments were paid. The situation cost Cervantes the loss of his daughter. Isabel never forgave him and cut off all contacts with her father.

As if Isabel wasn't enough of a problem for Cervantes, in November 1606, treasury agents renewed charges against him for unsettled accounts from his days as a tax collector. They demanded that he appear before them and pay his debts within 10 days. His explanations of the accounts were satisfactory and his indebtedness to the king finally settled.

By 1609, Cervantes and his wife could no longer afford to live on their own. His sisters once again shared his home to help with the rent.

As Cervantes grew older, he wrote in the prologue to the *Exemplary Novels*, "My age does not permit me to make light of the next life." He wanted to restore the relationship with the Catholic Church he had damaged while he was a commissary collecting supplies for the military. Twice the Catholic Church had excommunicated him in two different towns for taking supplies from churches.

His sister Andrea joined the St. Francis religious order on June 8, 1609. Their sister, Magdalena, had joined the order several months earlier. His wife Catalina joined the same order making her profession on June 27, 1610. In her will, made 11 days earlier, she mentioned "the great love and good company," she and Cervantes had given to each other. She also gave Cervantes the use of her property for life.

On April 17, 1609, Cervantes joined the Confraternity (Brotherhood) of the Most Holy Sacrament. This religious order run by Trinitarian friars was for laypeople, especially authors.

The order had strict rules for living. Cervantes had to attend Mass every day, wear religious garb, follow a strict regime of prayer and self-discipline, fast on prescribed days, and visit the sick. He followed these practices faithfully. The irony is that, in his writings, he made irreverent fun of the clergy and questioned some superstitious religious practices.

In 1610, Pedro Fernandez Ruiz de Castro y Osorio, seventh Count of Lemos, became Viceroy of Naples. As a patron of the arts, he planned to take a group of gifted literary men with him. Although it looked like the count was going to include Cervantes in the group headed for Italy, when Count Lemos left on July 3, Cervantes did not. Cervantes was devastated. He turned instead to his writing and poured his heart into the projects he had started.

Cervantes paid a brief visit to Alcalá in July 1613. While he was there, he visited the venerable Order of Franciscan Tertiaries and took their habit. This was an intermediate step in joining this lay order. Dissatisfied with the Trinitarian order, he withdrew from the Confraternity of the Most Holy Sacrament. In his view, it had become too secular and too heavily influenced by the aristocracy.

SPAIN'S GOLDEN AGE

Miguel de Cervantes lived during Spain's Golden Age. At this time, Spain excelled in education, art, and literature with the strong support from the royalty, especially King Philip II, the church, and the aristocrats. The University of Salamanca in central Spain was on the frontier of the study of economics and political theory. The University of Alcalá de Henares developed a strong reputation for biblical scholarship. One of the world's greatest painters, El Greco, flourished with his intensely emotional religious paintings. The plays of Lope de Vega and Pedro Calderon de la Barca y Henao were very popular and influenced other European playwrights. Miguel de Cervantes' novel *Don Quixote* became a high point of Spain's Golden Age and continues to be considered one of the best novels in world literature.

Cervantes visited his birthplace, Alcalá, in July 1613. There, he visited the Order of the Franciscan Tertiaries and took their habit, an initial step to joining this order. Although he had previously joined a Trinitarian brotherhood, Cervantes soon became disenchanted with the Trinitarian's secular concerns.

In the spring of 1616, Cervantes fell ill. His case was hopeless. However, he kept busy with his writing. In the prologue to *Persiles and Sigismunda* he referred to traveling 20 miles to and from Esquivias, most likely to take care of his wife's business. On his way back to Madrid, he wrote of meeting a young student riding on a donkey who caught up with Cervantes' party. The youth was impressed at meeting the famous author. The student rode with Cervantes, telling him that he was a medical student. Upon learning of Cervantes' physical condition he told Cervantes:

> Your trouble . . . is a dropsy, which not all the water of Ocean can cure. . . . Your Grace, Señor Cervantes, must drink next to nothing at all, at the same time not forgetting to eat. This will cure you without any other medicine.

Cervantes most likely had diabetes, an illness unknown at that time. Cervantes replied to the student:

> Many other people have told me that . . . as a matter of fact I can continue to drink at my ease as if I had been born for nothing else, for my life is running away. Judging by the daily rate of my pulses everything will be over by next Sunday. Your Grace has made my acquaintance in the nick of time, and I have not enough to show my gratitude for the interest you have taken in me.

The youth departed and Cervantes continued his journey home. Of course, no one knows whether this incident really happened.

When Cervantes wrote about the death of Don Quixote at the end of Part II, he may have anticipated his own death as well:

> As all human things, especially the lives of men, are transitory, being ever on the decline from their beginnings till they reach their final end, and as Don Quixote had no privilege from Heaven exempting him from the common fate, his dissolution and end came when he least expected it.

In his last days, Cervantes wrote:

> Goodbye, graces, goodbye, elegances! Goodbye, my jovial friends! For now I see myself approaching death and desiring to see you all before long, happy in the other life.

His parents and siblings had preceded him in death. His father died in June 1585 at age 75. His mother died in Madrid in October 1593, at age 73. His brother Rodrigo died tragically in battle in July 1600. His oldest sister, Andrea, who had joined a religious order, died a sudden death from a fever on October 9, 1609. His sister Magdalena died in January 1611 after being ill for several months. Finally, his granddaughter's death in 1610 had caused the end of his relationship with his daughter, Isabel.

Cervantes became too ill to leave his home. After three years as a novice, on April 2, 1616, he took final vows in the Franciscan order. The ceremony took place at his house. On April 18, he received an Extreme Unction (sacrament that gives strength to the deathly ill) from the licentiate Francisco Lopez. Lopez had given the last rites of the church to his two Franciscan sisters.

After receiving the sacrament, Cervantes lived for four more days. During that time he wrote his final words in the dedication of *Persiles* to Count Lemos, who had sponsored him. He wrote:

> With my foot now in the stirrup,
> And the hour of death at hand,
> Great Lord, (Count Lemos) I write this letter . . .
> Yesterday they gave me Extreme Unction, and today I
> am writing this. Time is short, my pains increase,
> my hopes wane; and yet I cling to life in my desire to
> live on . . .

The parish records of San Sebastian show that Miguel de Cervantes died on April 22, 1616, at age 69, with his wife at his side. He died about a week after the death of the famous English writer, William Shakespeare. He had 10 Masses said for his soul. The funeral Mass was said by the Franciscan friar who earlier had ransomed Cervantes from prison in Algiers. Following the Franciscan custom, he was buried in the Trinitarian monastery wearing his habit with his face uncovered.

His wife Catalina outlived him by 10 years. She died in October 1626. She was buried in the chapel of the Trinitarian nuns, near her husband.

Other members of his family died later. His sister Luisa, the Carmelite nun, died in 1620, in her seventies. Cervantes' niece, Constanza, who lived with him and his wife for some time, died unmarried in 1624. His daughter Isabel died in 1652, childless and engaged in several business disputes. It appears that she did win her fight with Urbina, since record books show that she sold his house.

There are no known descendants of Cervantes today.

Chronology

1547   Born Miguel de Cervantes in Alcalá de Henares, Spain.

1551   Family moves to Valladolid for a better life, but Rodrigo, Miguel's father, is imprisoned because of his debts and all family possessions are confiscated.

1553   Family returns to Alcalá de Henares; Cervantes may have attended Jesuit school in Córdoba.

1564   Father moves to Seville with one child, mother moves to Alcalá with the other children.

1566   Family moves to Madrid.

1568   Studies with Juan López de Hoyos, who refers to Cervantes as a "beloved pupil" and commissions him to write four poems.

1569   Cervantes leaves Spain for Rome, Italy, where he is a chamberlain to Monsignor Acquaviva. A possible explanation for Cervantes' unexpected move to Rome is to escape punishment for his involvement in a duel with Antonio de Sigura.

1571   Cervantes, ill with malaria, participates in the Battle of Lepanto against the Ottoman Turks, receiving two chest wounds and permanently damaging his left hand. His superiors declare him a war hero.

1572   In spite of losing the use of his left hand, he continues as a highly paid soldier for several years, taking part in various campaigns.

1575   Cervantes and his brother, Rodrigo, are captured by pirates and imprisoned in the North African city of Algiers. Cervantes' ransom is set at 500 gold *ducats*, an amount his family cannot afford to pay.

1576   Cervantes' first escape attempt with other Christians, who are abandoned by their Muslim guide and must return to prison.

1577 Rodrigo, Miguel's brother, is ransomed from prison and brings a boat to rescue Cervantes and 14 other prisoners. However, the plan does not work and Cervantes is returned to prison, claiming full responsibility for the escape. He is placed in the king's dungeon.

1578 Cervantes attempts a third escape by sending letters with a Muslim to the commander of Orán, asking for a spy to rescue them. The Muslim is arrested, and Cervantes is sentenced to harsh punishment, yet there is no record that punishment was administered.

1579 His fourth attempt at escape, a plan to board a frigate with 60 others, is thwarted and he is locked up.

1580 After five years in captivity, the Trinitarian Friars collect enough money, and Friar Juan Gil journeys to Algiers to pay Cervantes' ransom. Cervantes returns to Spain, where he unsuccessfully seeks a government post, and then develops relationships with well-known poets, launching his literary career.

1584 He has an affair with a friend, Ana Franca de Rojas, who gives birth to his only daughter, Isabel de Saavedra. He travels to Esquivas, where, at age 37, he marries the 19-year-old Catalina de Salazar.

1585 His father dies. Cervantes signs a contract for the publishing of two plays. His novel *La Galatea* is published.

1587 Cervantes obtains the post of Royal Commissioner of Supplies to purchase supplies for the Spanish Armada. It is the beginning of a 15 year period as a businessman. The time is filled with lawsuits, jail, and excommunication from the church.

1592 Cervantes signs contracts to write six plays.

1593 His mother dies. His commissioner of supplies job ends. He composes some poems, and he may have sketched some short novels.

1594   He becomes a tax collector.

1597   Imprisoned in the Seville jail for not paying money requested by a judge, he may have sketched the plot for his novel *Don Quixote*.

1605   His novel, *The Ingenious Gentleman Don Quixote de la Mancha*, is published in Madrid and becomes an instant success. A man is killed in front of his house, and he and his family are jailed for a brief time as part of an investigation into the circumstances leading to the murder.

1609   Worried about his salvation, he joins the congregation of the Confraternity of the Most Holy Sacrament.

1612   Now famous as a novelist, he joins fashionable literary academies.

1614   Cervantes publishes *Journey to Parnassus*. A false *Don Quixote Part II* appears in print.

1615   Cervantes' Part II of *Don Quixote* is published.

1616   Incurably ill, he takes final vows in the Third Order of Saint Francis, a religious order he joined three years earlier. On April 18 he receives the last rites. On April 22 Cervantes dies.

1617   *The Labors of Persiles and Sigismunda*, completed just before his death, is published posthumously.

Bibliography

Adler, Mortimer J. and Seymour Cain. *Imaginative Literature II from Cervantes to Dostoevsky.* Chicago: Encyclopedia Brittanica, Inc., 1962.

Busoni, Rafaello. *The Man Who Was Don Quixote: The Story of Miguel de Cervantes.* Englewood Cliffs, N.J.: Prentice Hall, Inc., 1958.

Bryon, William. *Cervantes: A Biography.* New York: Doubleday, 1978.

Canavaggio, Jean. *Cervantes.* New York: W.W. Norton & Co., 1990.

Cervantes Saavedra, Miguel de. *The Adventures of Don Quixote.* Translation by J. M.Cohen. New York: Viking Penquin, Inc., 1950.

Cruz, Anne J. and Carroll B. Johnson, eds. *Cervantes and His Postmodern Constituencies.* New York: Garland Publishing, Inc., 1999.

Diaz-Plaja, Fernando. *Cervantes: The Life Of A Genius.* New York: Charles Scribner's Sons, 1970.

Duran, Manuel. *Cervantes.* Boston: Twayne Publishers, 1974.

Goldberg, Jake. *Miguel de Cervantes.* New York: Chelsea House Publishers, 1993.

Ledesma, Francisco Navarro. *Cervantes: The Man and the Genius.* New York: Charterhouse, 1973.

Lewis, D. B. Wyndham. *The Shadow of Cervantes.* New York: Sheed & Ward, 1962.

Marlowe, Stephen. *The Death and Life of Miguel de Cervantes: a Novel.* New York: Arcade Publishing, 1991.

McKendrick, Melveena. *Cervantes.* Boston: Little, Brown, 1980.

Milton, Joyce. *Miguel de Cervantes' Don Quixote: Barron's Book Notes.* New York: Barron's Educational Series, Inc., 1985.

Mondadori, Arnoldo. *Cervantes: His Life, His Times, His Works.* New York: American Heritage Press, 1970.

Newcomb, Covelle. *Vagabond In Velvet. The Story of Miguel de Cervantes.* New York: David McKay Company, Inc., 1942.

Predmore, Richard L. *Cervantes.* New York: Dodd, Mead & Company, 1973.

Russell, P. E. *Cervantes.* New York: Oxford University Press, 1985.

Websites

The Center for Cervantes Studies
www.csdl.tamu.edu/cervantes/english/cec.html

Don Quixote Exhibit
http://quixote.mse.jhu.edu/

Coloquio, The Electronic Newspaper of the Hispanic Community
http://coloquio.com/

The Cervantes Project
http://www.csdl.tamu.edu/cervantes

The Don Quixote Portal
http://www.donquixote.com

Further Reading

Canavaggio, Jean. *Cervantes*. New York: W.W. Norton & Co., 1990.

Cervantes Saavedra, Miguel de. *The Adventures of Don Quixote*. Translation by J. M. Cohen. New York: Viking Penquin, Inc., 1950.

Diaz-Plaja, Fernando. *Cervantes: The Life Of A Genius*. New York: Charles Scribner's Sons, 1970.

Goldberg, Jake. *Miguel de Cervantes*. New York: Chelsea House Publishers, 1993.

Marlowe, Stephen. *The Death and Life of Miguel de Cervantes: a Novel*. New York: Arcade Publishing, 1991.

McCrory, Donald. *No Ordinary Man: The Life and Times of Miguel de Cervantes*. London: Peter Owen Ltd., 2002.

McKendrick, Melveena. *Cervantes*. Boston: Little, Brown, 1980.

Milton, Joyce. *Miguel de Cervantes' Don Quixote: Barron's Book Notes*. New York: Barron's Educational Series, Inc., 1985.

Newcomb, Covelle. *Vagabond In Velvet: The Story of Miguel de Cervantes*. New York: David McKay Company, Inc., 1942.

Predmore, Richard L. *Cervantes*. New York: Dodd, Mead & Company, 1973.

Index

Picture Credits

About the Authors

Barbara Keevil Parker and **Duane F. Parker** live and work in Riverside, Rhode Island. Among Barbara's published books are *North American Wolves* and *Susan B. Anthony: Daring to Vote*. She is the author of numerous articles for children's periodicals and professional journals. Barbara is an instructor with the Institute of Children's Literature and a licensed marriage and family therapist.

Duane's articles on religion, theology, and mental health have appeared in professional journals and monographs. He has also published poetry and served as newsletter editor. Duane was a Heritage Fellow for historical study at Old Deerfield, Massachusetts.

Barbara and Duane earned their B.A.s from the University of Puget Sound, and their Ph.D.s from Kansas State University. Duane also has a M.Div. from Garrett Evangelical Theological Seminary.